A Brief History of God

Other Books by Terry Austin

- *My Two Fathers: What My Earthly Father Taught me About my Heavenly Father*

- *Why I Quit Going to Church*

- *Broken: The Life and Times of Erik Daniels*

- *Acceptance, Forgiveness, and Love: Building a Church Without Fences*

- *Intermission*

- *Authentic Stewardship*

- *Christmas Parables*

- *Treasure Hunting*

- *Financial Truth*

- *Successful Christian Money Management*

- *Partners With God: Bible Truths About Giving*

A Brief History of God

A Better Understanding of Love and Forgiveness

Terry Austin

Austin Brothers

— PUBLISHING —
www.abpbooks.com

A Brief History of God
A Better Understanding of Love and Forgiveness

Terry Austin

Published by Austin Brothers Publishing, Fort Worth, Texas
www.abpbooks.com

Scripture quotations taken from the (NASB®) New American Standard Bible®, Copyright © 1960, 1971, 1977, 1995, 2020 by The Lockman Foundation. Used by permission. All rights reserved. www.lockman.org

ISBN: 978-1-7375807-6-8

Printed in the United States of America
2022 -- First Edition

To my father

He would not agree with all of the conclusions of this book, but he taught me to be an independent thinker, which led to these conclusions. He also showed me that we could talk about our differences and continue to love one another even if we didn't agree.

but more importantly...

To Sharon

She patiently listened to my questions and refused to allow me to have easy answers as we walked together on the journey that led to this book. Sharon has always been my best friend. For the past decade, she has been my caretaker. Most of all, she has been my mentor while writing this book.

Contents

Foreword

Having grown up in the church, I thought I had everything figured out about God. I had listened to sermon after sermon and heard the pastor tell me everything I thought I needed to know. After becoming dissatisfied with church and having questions about some of the basics I had learned, I began investigating by reading. I found some other people who were feeling the same way. I first met Terry Austin on social media. I read some of his articles and books, quickly learning that Terry was one of those people.

Terry and I got acquainted through our mutual writings about God. Because of his many books and posts, along with my ten years of blogging about life outside religion, we developed a mutual respect for one another. We have found that we have similar thoughts about church and religion, and many of those thoughts are not the traditional understanding.

Terry is well informed in religion and church matters. He has been writing in some form or fashion most of his life. Besides the twenty-five-plus books he has written himself, he specializes in ghost-writing and has helped more than one hundred others in their writing experience.

Terry was educated in a Christian college and seminary and spent many years in the church specializing in stewardship and finances; also a co-pastor and a pastor. He has plenty of knowledge and experience in the Christian life. Through these experiences, he has come up with some interesting views and insights into the basics of God. Terry is able to express his knowledge in an extremely interesting, informative, yet simple way with some humor thrown in along the way.

The book you are about to read gives great insight into what we have been taught about God in the early years of our religious experience. Terry's writing style will hold your attention and will make you think in new ways about God's love and purpose for humanity.

His writing covers many topics of the Bible and raises some good questions about what we thought we knew about God. I can honestly say that this book will raise good questions and possibly lead you to a new understanding of your faith.

When I thought I had all the answers and had God all figured out, Terry's writing made me wonder if I may have been mistaken about some of my views. I began to think about God in new and interesting ways.

If you have been in church for a while, are just starting out, or left church attendance, this book will help clear up some questions and misconceptions about God. It will also provide information that will give you a clearer understanding of who God is and what He desires for us.

As someone who grew up in the church and has been writing about God, I greatly appreciate Terry Austin and his writing style. Terry has a way of expressing his thoughts about God in a way we all can understand. Like me, once you finish this book, you will come away with a better view of God and his love for all of us.

Jim Gordon, Done with Religion
https://donewithreligion.com

Introduction

When it was first published, I read Stephen Hawking's book, *A Brief History of Time*. It was 1988, and I was still young and believed I could figure out anything with enough effort. After reading the entire book, cover to cover, I can testify that I understood five, maybe six pages. That's about the level of understanding I expected. The primary reason for reading the book was not to gain a new appreciation of time but to support a fellow wheelchair user. I'll give it to Hawking when it comes to physics, but I had a few years of experience on him when it came to wheelchairs.

If he can write a brief history of time, why can't I write a brief history of God? I'm not sure where this will take us, but I'm confident it will be a shorter treatise than Hawking produced, although, if I remember correctly, his wasn't a large book.

This essay will not be heavily footnoted because nobody reads footnotes anyway. However, under oath, if you desire, I can testify that I have read through the entire Bible numerous times. At various times over the years, I have memorized large portions of Scripture, so I have spent a great deal of time trying to understand God.

I've also had a good deal of experience writing biographies of other people. These stories have included a small-town doctor, a Canadian billionaire, a woman sold into slavery by her mother, a Washington trial lawyer, a wounded vet, a woman married to a sociopath for 30 years, and a few others. None of these people provided as much information as I have about God, so I can do this.

The most fascinating biography I wrote was the story of a young man who was born into a world of violence and abuse. As a juvenile, he killed his grandfather, who had been sexually abusing him for years, by stabbing him dozens of times. He got involved in drugs, not only using but also selling. He flew drugs from Columbia to Arizona in small planes and was heavily connected with major dealers.

When caught by the DEA, he became a witness and had to live the rest of his life in hiding. During that time, he killed two other people to protect his identity. Although he trusted me to write his life story, he never trusted me with his identity. I have no idea what his real name might be. Or should I say, might have been? He died about two-thirds of the way through the process, and I had to write the last couple of chapters based on what he had told me in earlier interviews.

He called himself Erik Daniels, and you might be wondering why I bring him up when I'm writing about God. Hang with me; Erik will show up again in God's story and play a crucial role in making sense of the divine.

I need to clarify a few other things before we head down the biography path. You must know that I don't think science threatens my Christian faith. I'm sure you figured that out when I told you I read a book by Stephen Hawking. Science has always caused me to think even though I do not consider science a strong subject. If I'm playing *Jeopardy* and the Final Category is Science, you can be sure that my wager will be very low.

When I was in second or third grade, we moved from a small town in the Colorado mountains to a large city, or at least it was large by my standards. I remember the first couple of days of school, hearing the teacher and some of the other kids talk about someone named Mother Nature. I had never heard of her before. As I listened to them talk, I concluded that Mother Nature was God's wife. They kept talking about the things she did, and they were the same things I thought God did, so they must be working together.

If you say the earth is millions of years old, that's not a problem for me. I'm not sure how you or anyone else knows that, but it's not a threat to my faith or understanding of God. This doesn't mean I don't think God is the creator. When it comes to creation, the Bible is the place to go for who and why but not for how—that's the role of science.

It also means I would never say, "evolution is devilution." Accepting that fossils are real is much easier than finding other ways to explain where they came from. Although I've never been fascinated with dinosaurs like kids are today, I don't deny they existed.

Christians have a difficult time with science because their God is too small. For many, if dinosaurs were real, then God is not, or if evolution happens, God is a fraud. They need a bigger God. Using the term "bigger" is not a reference to physical size.

When asked to describe God, most people begin with the image of an old grey-haired man living up in the sky. He has features, just like a grandpa, only he's really strong and in good health. If you tell them their God is not big enough, they're likely to think that God needs to bulk up, kind of like the Incredible Hulk or Hulk Hogan with a full head of hair.

When I suggest the need for a bigger God, I reference the need to stop thinking of God in human form. God is spirit; He is not physical. God does not consist of cells. God is not in any way human. That means he doesn't have a gender, race, religion, family heritage, or culture. We use human terms when we speak of God, but that's only because we have no other language.

To speak of God as spirit suggests that He is like an unseen energy that permeates the universe. The Psalmist expressed this idea when writing, "Where could I go from your presence..." (Psalm 139.7). God is not sitting up in heaven, wherever that might be, moving the pieces of the universe like a chess master. He is right here, in the air we breathe, the ground we walk on, and, as we will see later, within us.

Once again, understanding the limits of language, stop visualizing God as a strong man, or a woman for the feminists, and picture God as more like a vapor. God is not a liquid or a solid but more like a mist or steam. In a steam-filled room like a sauna, the steam is all around, in every crevice. God is like that. The universe is the sauna, and God is the mist or vapor. (Although I said earlier that science is not my strong suit, I do know the difference between mist and vapor, but they have enough similarities to make the analogy work.)

We can push the analogy further by suggesting the vapor that represents God is some type of energy. I know this is starting to sound like some *Star Trek* thing, but it shows how difficult it is to explain the unexplainable. Picture an energy you can't see that is really an energy permeating everything in the universe, and I think we are getting closer to describing God.

This imagery allows us to understand how God is not confined by space or time. It provides a God who existed before and during the period of the dinosaurs; a God present for the millions of years or whatever it took for evolution; or the billions of years required for some type of Big Bang to occur (more on that later). Understanding God as a spirit allows for a God big enough to be whatever God needs to be.

However, how do you write the history of something you can't see, hear, taste, smell, or feel? It's not easy making sense of something you can't encounter with any of your senses. Earlier, I referenced the inspiration for my title was Stephen Hawking. He took on the same task as he wrote *The History of Time*. You can see, hear, feel, and taste a clock (not likely to smell) but not time. If I recall from that book, he talked a great deal about black holes and other spaces that are theoretically accepted as existing.

I don't accept the existence of God as a solid theory. It's a matter of faith. In fact, it might be the definition of faith – knowing something you can't see, touch, hear, taste, or smell is real. Hebrews 11:1 says, "Faith is the substance of things hoped for, the evidence of things not seen."

Faith is the *substance* of our hopes. The word translated *faith* (or sometimes *certainty*) is interesting. If you watch crime shows on television, you've probably heard the coroner declare the person was not killed where the body was found, and the evidence is *hypostasis*. It means when the body dies; fluid settles in the lowest spots. When the body is moved, it's obvious because the fluid settled in a different part of the body. When the fluid settles at the foundation, that's *hypostasis*. Faith is the *hypostasis* (foundation) of our hopes.

Faith is also the *evidence* of things not observed by any of our five senses, in other words, the evidence of God. Again, another significant term. This one comes from the Socratic teaching method when the teacher doesn't impart information but asks pointed questions that guide the student. The result is a deeper understanding because the student discovered the solution. This is how we find evidence for God.

Thus, before me lies an impossible task—write a history of someone I can't see, touch, hear, taste, or smell. This is compounded by the reality that every other person already has an opinion about this subject that might, but probably not, agree with mine. So, I begin with what I consider the most concrete thing we can know about God, His desire to relate to the world He has created and especially the most unique part of that creation, humans. I think that is the clearest thing we know about God, and it has been expressed repeatedly since the beginning.

That is the thesis of this book – God's desire to have fellowship with humans. If we don't understand this, we will never understand God. To miss this truth causes us to view the Bible as a history book that records dates and facts, or a science book that explains how the world works, or a rule book that lists what needs to be done to be accepted. The Bible is a **relationship** book that repeatedly explains how God loves us (all of us) and wants to fellowship with us.

Part 1: God's Desire Expressed through Revelation

What we know about another person is limited by what they have chosen to reveal to us. I thought I knew my wife when we were married, but after 47 years together, I know far more about her. She has allowed me to see more facets of her personality. I know what she likes, what she fears, how she thinks, and what she desires. I could write a book about Sharon, but I know she wouldn't like that. I've never asked her, but I know her well enough there's no need to ask.

Just like I could write a book about my wife because she has revealed herself to me, I can write a book about God because of His self-revelation. Humans would know nothing about God were it not for divine revelation. We are totally dependent on God for existence, not only in origin but also in continuation. If we pay attention, we can learn much about God from looking around at the universe (thank you, Stephen Hawking), reading historical records (biblical and non-biblical), relating to other people, and searching deep within ourselves. God can be found in all of these.

Part One will answer three questions. First, how do we know? There are some proven methods for gleaning information, and we will examine what they are and how they work. The second question is, what do we know? In other words, what does revelation teach us about God and the desire to be in a relationship with humans?

The final question of this section searches for an answer that has plagued humans since the beginning. In fact, we're going to go back to the beginning to discover what went wrong, our final question.

How Do We Know?

I have written numerous books for other people, and many of those fall into the category of a memoir. I don't know if this is a classical understanding, but to me, a memoir is written from the subject's perspective, whereas a biography is written by an observer. Writing a memoir for someone else is not difficult if you can get them to talk. My process begins with extensive interviews, getting them to talk about their life and experiences. After hearing their story, I then search other resources to clarify or verify the subject's memory.

Writing a biography does not require the subject's involvement. Often, the subject is deceased, so there is no way to tap their memory. It's good to find writing, tapes, or videos made by the subject, but they are not always available. In that case, the biography must be constructed from third-party resources—what did others say about the person, what is recorded in history.

This work is not God's memoir; it's a *Brief History of God*. It is more like a biography for one simple reason. God is not available for an interview. Many Christians speak of "talking with God," but it's a one-sided conversation if they're honest. It would be nice if we could sit down for an extended conversation; I have many questions. I can ask the questions, but it's not likely God will answer them. Consequently, I'm left with writing a biography as if God is dead, even though that's not true.

I realize some have suggested that God is dead or never existed in the first place. We even have a name for these people—we call them atheists. Based on my understanding of humans, I don't believe a real atheist exists.

To find evidence that atheists don't exist, I went to the source. The website of the organization that identifies itself as "American Atheists" provides this definition: "To be clear: Atheism is not a disbelief in Gods or a denial of Gods; it is a lack of belief in Gods."

As an experienced writer, if I handed this sentence to an editor, I would expect it to be returned with the question, "What the hell does this mean?"

Those who claim to be atheists essentially say they don't believe in our God or anybody's God. They have yet to find a description of

A Better Understanding of Love and Frogiveness

God that meets what they define as necessary for God. If they are honest, most atheists don't believe in a particular God.

The biggest obstacle to atheism is there is no way to explain the created world without God. They are left with the doctrine that everything in this complex world exists because of random chance. Have they never watched a nature documentary on the Smithsonian Network?

Now the question is simple: What do we know about this God?

Believe it or not, I can remember the first Systematic Theology course I took in college and in seminary. The outline for both was essentially the same since they were both affiliated with Baptists. The first theological issue is revelation. Revelation is the study of the self-disclosure of God. In other words, how do we know God exists, and how do we know anything about God.

If I remember the terms correctly, all revelation can be divided into two categories—general and special. General revelation refers to the information about God that is available to everyone. It doesn't require any scripture or momentary apparition by God. It describes what we can know about God by looking around at the universe. What do we know about God by studying the stars and planets, the land and the oceans, and the fish and animals?

Special revelation is sometimes labeled as direct revelation and speaks of God's unique self-revelation through appearance, speech, and even written word. Within the Christian tradition, it would mean the scriptures, visions like Isaiah in the temple or John on the isle of Patmos, and even direct speech and action like Moses receiving the commandments.

To write a history of God, having good sources of information is crucial. A biographer of a historical person is not able to speak with the subject personally, so the writer studies their writing and speeches, reads what others have said about the person, and digs into historical records.

Page 11

General Revelation: Telescopes and Microscopes

I remember camping trips in the Colorado mountains and peering up at the sky on a dark night. The abundance of stars was amazing. I learned later that what I could see, even when away from city lights, was only a fraction of the stars that exist. It might be considered circumstantial evidence in a court of law, but it does point to a creator God of some kind. That's General Revelation.

If you have ever struggled with believing that God exists, I recommend you visit a planetarium. Lean back in the over-padded seat and adjust your eyes to the darkness of the room. As you look up at the imaginary sky, the narrator will clearly explain various facets of the stars and planets that make up our solar system. Then you're likely to hear that the vastness of our solar system includes more than 3,000 stars, in addition to our Sun, with planets in orbit. Even these are only a portion of the billion stars in the universe.

Then you might hear that if the rotation of the earth, our home, was slightly altered to move closer or further away from the Sun, life would be impossible. We are not the result of a cosmic accident. Ever since Galileo peered at the planets and stars through the newly invented telescope in the 17th century, it has been obvious the world is far more expansive than early humans ever envisioned.

> *The heavens tell of the glory of God;*
> *And their expanse declares the work of His hands.*
> *Day to day pours forth speech,*
> *And night to night reveals knowledge.* (Psalm 19:1-2)

"For since the creation of the world His invisible attributes, that is, His eternal power and divine nature, have been clearly perceived, being understood by what has been made, so that they are without excuse." (Romans 1:20)

If looking to the heavens does not convince you, peer into the most powerful microscopes. Study the inner workings of the human body. Try to understand DNA and how these microscopic strands determine our every characteristic. The size of your nose, crooked big toe, and the way you laugh are predetermined by genes passed from one generation to the next. You are not a cosmic accident.

The clearest proof that general revelation is real is that every tribe on the planet has a concept of God. I'm not suggesting that every person who has ever lived believed that God exists; there have always been atheists. However, there has not been a tribe discovered that did not have some understanding of what we call God. Some of the more ancient cultures taught the existence of multiple gods.

Ancient Greeks, Native Americans in the northern plains, primitive tribes in the Brazilian rain forest, and every other culture, large and small, have a concept of God derived from observing nature.

Special Revelation: Scripture

In order to write a history of God, having good sources of information is crucial. Since the biographer of a historical person is not able to speak with the subject personally, the writer studies their writing and speeches, reads what others have said about the person, and digs into historical records.

> The B-I-B-L-E, yes, that's the book for me.
> I stand alone on the Word of God,
> The B-I-B-L-E.
> (*One of the earliest songs I learned as a child*)

Like many Christians, I strive to read the Bible every day. However, I admit to frequent failures and that I'm not as diligent as in times past. I remember the first time I set out to read the entire book, from Genesis to Revelation. I was working the graveyard shift as a police dispatcher. There was usually a lot of downtime after three in the morning. I carried my Bible with me and read during those stretches and finished in a few months. When I was a pastor, I tried to read through the entire Bible every year, not always successfully.

I have given the Bible a lot of influence in my life but not nearly as much as some. I don't worship the Bible. Many Christians, or should I say "most" Christians, have the opinion that the Bible is the "Word of God." Let me say up front, the Bible is not the word of God.

In the familiar opening words of the Gospel of John, the identification of Jesus as the Word of God is clearly laid out. "In the beginning was the Word, and the Word was with God, and the Word was God" (John 1:1). There is no way those words apply to a book. Later, John adds, "and the Word became flesh, and dwelt among us; and we saw his glory, glory as of the only Son from the Father, full of grace and truth" (John 1:14). Then he described how John, the evangelist baptizing people in the wilderness, made it clear that Jesus was the Word of God.

When you read the Bible from this perspective, you will find that it makes much more sense. Every time you encounter the phrase "Word of God," substitute Jesus.

Hebrews 4:12 - *For the word of God (JESUS) is alive and active. Sharper than any double-edged sword, it penetrates even to dividing soul and spirit, joints and marrow; it judges the thoughts and attitudes of the heart.*

Psalm 119:105 - *Your word (JESUS) is a lamp for my feet, a light on my path.*

Luke 11:28 - *He replied, "Blessed rather are those who hear the word of God (JESUS) and obey it."*

Psalm 33:4 - *For the word of the Lord (JESUS) is right and true; he is faithful in all he does.*

James 1:21 - *Therefore, get rid of all moral filth and the evil that is so prevalent and humbly accept the word (JESUS) planted in you, which can save you.*

That raises the question if the Bible is not the word of God, what is the Bible. Let me begin by saying that the Bible makes Christianity (and Judaism) different from all other major religions of the world. Buddhism and Hinduism do not have a sacred text that guides their belief and actions. Islam has the Koran, but it is significantly different from the Bible. It was written by one man over a short period of time, 20 years in the 7th century. Although it's not a major world religion, Mormonism uses the Bible along with the sacred Book of Mormon written by one man in the 19th century (although he claims they were written much earlier and miraculously given to him).

Judaism and Christianity are similar when it comes to sacred writings. In fact, Christianity incorporates the writings of Judaism into its Bible as the Old Testament to go along with the New Testament. However, the composition of both the Old and New Testaments are similar. They are both a collection of material composed over a long period, written by a plethora of authors.

I don't think any of the biblical writers thought they were writing God's words. Instead, they were writing what they knew, what they heard, and what they experienced about God. **The Bible is a collection of words about God, not a collection of God's words to us.**

We don't know who wrote down the words of scripture. Historically, names have been ascribed to various books and portions, but we know they are not always accurate. For example, many people claim that Moses wrote the first five books of the Old Testament—Genesis, Exodus, Leviticus, Numbers, and Deuteronomy. That is hard to be true since a description of Moses' death is contained in those writings. A few books of the Bible claim to have been written by a specific individual. Others were named after a likely individual, and others are simply unknown.

The Bible was written by humans who took the occasion to put down on paper (or parchment or whatever they used at the time) their experience with God. The experiences were varied for many reasons. They happened at different times to people with different personalities and interests. Sometimes they are consistent with one another, but often they are in conflict.

The early chapters of Genesis contain two versions of the creation stories. At different times, God instructs his people to destroy all the enemy, and at other times He tells them not to. It seems God wanted Saul to be the king, except when He didn't intend for the nation to have a king. The list of inconsistencies found throughout the Bible is long.

You find them even in the New Testament. After being baptized, Jesus spent 40 days in the wilderness being tempted by Satan, yet three days after his baptism, Jesus was at a wedding in Cana.

To keep the Bible from contradicting itself, scholars have used a lot of ink along with some creative reasoning to explain how these are not inconsistencies. They feel compelled to do this because to believe the Bible is God's Word; it must not contradict itself. God would never say one thing and then later say something else. Scholars have even argued that the Bible is without error in the "original documents," which, of course, we don't have and never will.

Whew, that was close. Now it's ok if the Bible contradicts itself. We can blame the scribes who came along throughout history and made copies. Someone made a tiny mistake, and after being copied and recopied countless times, some mistakes became large. But that's ok; God's Word was perfect when given. Humans messed it up.

Even if I accept that reasoning, how does that help me? If the Bible is God's Word, but we no longer have large portions of that Word, it feels like we might be missing something important. I guess you could say that God made sure we preserved the important parts, but now you're just guessing; there's no way to know that.

There has to be a better way than trying to make the Bible into something it's not. Rather than being God's Word to humans, the Bible is human words about God. The Bible is a collection of writings produced over time by men (and probably not women, sad to say). They recorded their experience of God and what that taught them about God.

I'm not saying their writings are not different than any of the dozens of books I've written over the years. They are vastly different. Paul understood this when he wrote, "All Scripture is inspired by God and profitable for teaching, for reproof, for correction, for training in righteousness" (2 Timothy 3:16). The phrase "inspired by God" is one word in the Greek language and means "God-breathed." It means that Scripture is "God's breath." As the author put pen to paper, God was breathing on the process. It doesn't say He dictated or spoke; he breathed. I'm not sure what that means or how much it impacted the final words, but it does make them special. Unlike anything you and I have ever produced.

I know a thing or two about breathing. As a result of polio since infancy, as an old man, I have difficulty breathing. The problem is with my diaphragm, which allows air to flow in and out of the lungs. Mine has been weakened over the years, and exhaling is difficult. It's not enough to breathe in. In order to live, we must inhale and exhale. I use a machine that compensates and makes it easier for me to breathe out.

God breathed into the writers of scripture, but that wasn't enough. Nothing was written or told until they breathed out. That's why the Bible isn't perfect, straight from God. It didn't come straight from God but was routed through humans. To say the scriptures are inspired by God does not mean they are perfect.

A further consideration is that God's people have agreed over the centuries that these documents are unique and deserve special consideration. History records the arduous task of finding a consensus on which writings were God-breathed and which were not. No one, not even me, considers that any of my writing is God-breathed.

I think I've gone far enough that I can now explain what I believe about the Bible. It is a collection of men's (again, it's a shame we have no women) experiences with God and what it meant to them. As these inspired men gathered the experiences and teachings passed down to them from others, it was all lumped together with community legends and folklore and put together with the breath of God. In other words, scripture is not God's word; it is men's words about God.

All of this material, woven together by God over the centuries, was further edited by people's usage until church leaders eventually got together, debated, voted, and declared, "this is the Bible."

By the way, it is still being edited. When was the last time you took a deep dive into the Song of Solomon? How often do you read the book of Jude?

With this book, which I'm calling *A Brief History of God*, I'm attempting to do something similar. It is a description of God based on my experience and informed by many who have gone before me. However, I make no claim that it is "God-breathed" in any manner.

We have revelation through nature and scripture, but now we need to know what's true. If we admit that looking at the stars convinces us that God exists, we still don't know much about him. We can't see, feel, smell, hear, or taste God, so there's little comfort in just believing in the existence of God. We need more. Then we read scripture; for the Christian, that's the Bible. Even that's confusing. The Bible contradicts itself frequently, and it's not a stretch to say the God described in the Old Testament seems far different from the one in the New Testament.

There is still much to do in our quest to know God's history.

What Do We Know? – It Started with a Bang

It was an unlikely conversation with a building contractor. Rick supervised the construction of an addition to our church building, and we often talked about various subjects. He was not what I expected when we first met. In addition to being a good carpenter, he was a resource for high school science and math teachers when they confronted a question they couldn't answer. He knew much more about both of those subjects than me.

Rick identified himself as an atheist, so it was somewhat unusual that all our conversations occurred in a church building. I think he called himself an atheist because he thought he was smarter than most Christians; too smart to believe in God. In our conversations, he proudly asserted that the world was not created by God; it was the result of a collision of pre-earth matter, creating a massive explosion that eventually settled, after perhaps billions of years, and became the universe as we know it.

At that point in our conversation, his previous experience with Christians was that they would get angry and insist he was crazy, saying it was easier to believe in God. When I didn't disagree with his theory, he was caught off guard. I kept pushing him back further.

"Who created the elements that collided?" I asked.

He suggested they evolved from other elements, so I pushed further. "Ok, who created those elements?"

He realized I could play that game forever, so he gave up. I could do that because my God was bigger than the God of many Christians.

As soon as you lock into the words of Genesis 1 to explain how God created, you have put yourself in a box. God created in an organized manner according to a time frame. Consequently, you have to argue against any suggestion or scientific evidence to the contrary.

Remember, the Bible, even the creation story, is one person's perception of what God did—He created. I suspect the story developed over generations of people gathered around tribal fires telling stories trying to make sense of the world. Genesis 1 is a good story that answers the questions of who and why, but it doesn't say anything about how. That's not a task for faith; that's a job for science. I allowed Rick to explain the how of creation, but he was unwilling to accept my explanation of who and why.

The writer of Genesis uses the creation story to explain the who and why of creation. The "who" is simple. In the beginning, God created the heavens and the earth. There can be no doubt about that. If there is to be a creation, there must be a creator.

Yes, I referred to it as the creation story. It is a story. A story is an account of persons or events that might be real or not. Stories come in fiction and non-fiction. Most stories are a combination. You and I could witness the same event, but when we go to tell the story of what we saw, they might not sound like the same event. Try telling a story with your wife listening, and you'll realize how little you observed.

The creation story was developed over a long time. There were no eyewitnesses. Remember, faith is concerned with who and why, not how. What we know from the creation story is who. God created, and if you read the two Genesis accounts, the why is also evident. We'll get to that shortly.

This is the story fashioned by the biblical writer:

The point of the story in Genesis 1 is the creation of humans. God, of course, is the protagonist, but the purpose is to tell us how a living, breathing human being came to exist. When it says, "In the beginning," we can read it as the beginning of the story of man.

First, it says that God created the heavens and the earth. We often get confused because we use the word in two different ways. We speak of "heaven" as the dwelling place of God, a spiritual realm. It is the place where God exists, and since God had no beginning, the realm of His existence had no beginning. The other use of "the heavens," from a human standpoint, is the blue sky above us, at least for ancient man. However, we now know "the heavens" are extensive, stretching for billions of miles and growing continually.

The "earth" is described as "without form and void." Perhaps the best way to understand is with the word "chaos." The earth existed, but it was a barren, useless wasteland shrouded in darkness. We must not forget that the Bible was written by ancient men of faith who had a completely different concept of the metaphysical world. They wrote with concrete terms, all they had at their disposal. The writers did not have the advantage of 21st-century science, but they were unconcerned with how it happened. They wrote to describe who and why.

For those who insist the Bible proves that God created in seven precise days, notice that it says the separation of the land and water happened on the "second day" (Genesis 1:8), but there were not yet any days to measure. There was no sun. The sun and moon that designate time did not exist.

With heaven and the earth in place, it was time for the pinnacle of God's creation. Like expecting a new baby with a fully stocked, lovingly designed nursery, it was time. God took a lump of fresh soil from the earth He recently created, shaped it, and breathed divine life into human lungs for the first time. It was the breath of God that made the human different from all other creatures.

Before you stress out and remind me that the name "Adam" means mankind and references all of humanity, I know that. But let me remind you that the biblical writer is telling a story, not reciting historical facts. The story is important because it explains everything we need to know about God and humans.

His first moment of self-consciousness for Adam was an amazing experience. He was already fully grown, no childhood to rely on. The world was pristine. His eyes saw nothing but the wonder of God's creation, freshly formed by the Word of God Himself.

This very first man, Adam, would be a great interview for any reporter. He possessed knowledge that has baffled all of us. I don't know about you, but I would really like to know what it was like to be the first human being. Imagine waking up on that initial day and finding yourself thrust into a beautiful garden filled with perfection.

As Adam focused his eyes on that original morning of life, the sun illuminated a sight that had never been seen by another human being. He was the first person to see the world that God had created. Rolling hills covered with flourishing green grass; trees laden with plump fruit shimmering with drops of water from the morning dew; the golden sun against the brilliant blue backdrop of the daylight sky; he experienced it all.

If anyone ever had an identity crisis, it was Adam. His first thoughts had to be, "Who am I?" and "What am I doing here?" He had no memory, no language, no history, no relationships. He was just there. In the most beautiful place ever created, he found himself all alone.

He was not all alone, really. God was there. It was God's custom, during the cool of the day, to spend time with His new creation. It happened so often that Adam recognized the sound of God moving through the garden (see Genesis 3:8). This relationship between God and Adam was a picture of intimacy – the Creator and His creation enjoying one another without any barriers.

Perhaps it was during these times together that God noticed something missing from Adam. He realized that it was not good for Adam to be alone (see Genesis 2:18), so He decided to act. First, He paraded all the animals that populated the garden in front of Adam for close inspection. Adam studied them and named them, which must have been an astonishing afternoon, exceeding any experience at the zoo we can imagine.

It was apparent to both God and Adam that none of the creatures could fill the empty void in Adam's life. No animal, despite its perfection or uniqueness, had the ability to be a partner to the crowning glory of God's creation. God had to do something.

He anesthetized Adam. Flat on his back in the wide-open spaces of the Garden of Eden, Adam became the first surgery patient. Why didn't God simply take some of the rich soil of the garden and create a woman as He did when He breathed life into Adam (see Genesis 2:7)? Why was Adam required to experience such painful surgery in order to have a partner? (If you have ever had a broken rib, you know the pain.)

The fact that woman was fashioned from the rib of man provides an important lesson about relationships. Something is missing from man's existence that can only be provided through a relationship with woman. No animal or object is sufficient to meet this need in man's life. Although some would have us believe that men are from Mars and women are from Venus, the truth is that we are a part of each other. We were created to need one another to be complete. (Another warning: Don't get your panties in a bunch about the gay thing. That's a subject for a different book.)

When he awoke in the recovery room of Eden, imagine his thoughts when his eyes first fell upon the woman. These were not the shouts and catcalls of a construction crew hurled at a woman walking down the sidewalk, nor were they the whistles and howls of a drunken patron at an adult nightclub. His thoughts bordered on reverence and awe.

Adam pledged that he, and all men after him, should "cleave" to the woman (see Genesis 2:24). He instinctively knew that living in relationship with woman was best for everyone concerned.

At that moment, everything was exactly as God intended for His created world to be. Humans had everything they needed, and God's desire for a relationship was filled. But it did not last.

One other thing the story tells us is the value of humans in God's estimation. The human is presented as the crowning achievement in God's creation. It was the end, the final act. Once God created the human, creation was finished; nothing else needed to be done, so God rested. All creation occurring for more than a billion years reached its zenith with the human. The human is what God was doing all along. Sure, God could have done it instantaneously with a finger snap (metaphorically speaking), but another way was chosen. The slow way is often better, like heating up leftover pizza in the oven instead of the microwave—the cheese is cheesier.

The *why* of creation is that God wanted a human. Humans were created in God's image and given the task of ruling over the rest of creation. Once the human existed, God was finished and took the day off.

One of the most obvious things we notice about God is that He loved man from the beginning. Not only was the human, king of all creation, but also placed in a specially created garden to live. In addition, God created a companion, the woman, not wanting man to be alone. Occasionally, God would come by to visit with the humans.

Reading the next couple of chapters of Genesis, it seems God wanted humans for the purpose of a relationship. We are told that God showed up frequently for a visit, kind of like a friendly neighbor.

I'm now ready to make another pronouncement about God. He desires to have a relationship with humans. He went to great lengths to make it happen. Inestimable time before an eventual big bang started things rolling, then perhaps millions of years of evolution until He finally had a person capable of sharing his life with God. God was so proud of this new creature that He made a special place, an idyllic garden with everything necessary to sustain life.

I don't know why, but I'm a fan of the TV show *Naked and Afraid*. The show involves two people, usually a man and a woman, who are stripped naked and placed in a jungle or some remote place in the world. They are expected to remain for 21 days, and it's up to them to find shelter, food, and water. Many of these people do remarkably well when dealing with wild predators, biting insects, scorching sun, and occasionally a disappointing partner.

The garden provided by God to the first humans was nothing like that. There is no shortage of food or water, no threatening weather, or cantankerous partners, probably not even mosquitos. The only similarity between Adam and Eve and the people on TV is the naked part. God stepped up and provided everything for these people to survive. Sharing fellowship was important.

The importance of the relationship between God and humans helps us understand the purpose of the forbidden tree. The humans were allowed to do whatever they wanted except pick and eat the fruit from one tree. Not an orchard, one single, lone tree.

If God did not put this restriction out there, He would have never known if man's communion was legitimate or forced. There could be no satisfaction for God if man did not have a choice. The option to ignore God meant that fellowship was sweeter; it was what the human wanted. God was careful not to create some kind of Stockholm Syndrome where a man fell in love with his captor. God wanted humans' voluntary, free-will expression of love.

Once again, we learn something important about God. He did everything He could to make a relationship with the human possible. As we will discover throughout our *Brief History of God*, it's a quality that manifests itself frequently over time. Humans don't exist because of some cosmic explosion that ultimately evolved into a person. We exist because God desires our fellowship.

Perhaps it would be fair to say that God was lonely. Imagine that; God had a need that could only be fulfilled by a human. Do you understand how important that makes us? It's common to hear people confess how much they need God, but it's also accurate to say that God needs us. I could make my brief history of God even briefer by telling you this is the conclusion to all of history. Everything that God has done, before creation, during creation, and since creation, is to maintain a relationship with humans. Stick with me, and your life is going to get much more interesting.

What Went Wrong – The Human Walked Away

Every year at Christmas time, I wrote a seasonal story for many years. Normally, I read them to the family on Christmas Eve, and it became a tradition. After some time, I had opportunities to share the stories in other venues. I've written stuff for most of my life, but these stories have been the only time I tackled fiction.

One of the great things about fiction is that the writer creates the character, including physical attributes and personality, often becoming too involved. My favorite story involved a man about my age who lost his wife and granddaughter in a tragic accident. Being an emotional guy at times, especially as I have aged, I couldn't read the story without crying. My heart ached for a guy who didn't even exist.

Stories, even fictional stories, can be a powerful and excellent way to make a point. **They don't have to be true to be true.** The man in my Christmas story is not real but what he experienced was truly painful.

I don't believe the story of Adam and Eve is factually true, but I do believe what it reveals is true. I'm aware they do a lot with genealogy today, but I'm confident it's impossible to trace the human race back to a single man. It's not necessary. The story's meaning can still be grasped even if the characters are not named Adam and Eve. These fictional characters reveal what went wrong with God's perfect creation.

The humans were in the perfect situation to enjoy communion with God with only one restriction—the forbidden tree. As I indicated earlier, the tree was not there to tempt the humans; God didn't want them to taste the fruit. It wasn't a test; it was an opportunity to choose a relationship with God, not to be forced because no other options existed.

The storyteller does a masterful job of creating a plot that explains how the decision was made. It came down to the belief that something was missing. God put them in a perfect place with everything necessary for a good life, but they still felt something was missing, something more they could possess. They believed information was withheld because God didn't intend for them to have everything. In their desire to acquire that one last thing, they took the forbidden fruit.

The fruit did open their eyes to a new truth, but not one they wanted. The fruit gave them shame. For the first time, they experienced embarrassment. They became aware of their nakedness, so they covered themselves and hid from the presence of God. Of course, God found them and put them on the spot with a few piercing questions. This led to further problems. The man blamed the woman, and the woman blamed the deceiving serpent.

When it came time to pronounce a sentence, God cursed the serpent (Genesis 3:14) and the ground (Genesis 3:17). God did not curse the woman or the man, merely pointing out the consequences of their actions. Women would suffer pain giving birth (something that had never happened at that point), and men would have to toil the cursed ground with thorns and thistles. A final consequence is that the bodies of the humans would die, returning to the earth from which they came. These are the consequences of hiding from God.

Historically, the origin of sin has been traced back to this story by theologians, describing the creation of humans and the beginning of sin. I agree that it provides insight into sin, but the sin of Adam and Eve was not what is usually classified as sin by many today. I came across a sermon by some guy describing 24 sins committed by Adam and Eve in this short story; the biggest stretch was "gluttony" (must have been a huge fruit).

We typically define sin as breaking a rule. We begin with the Top Ten given to Moses. To disobey one of these rules is what we consider sin. Elaborate religious legal systems have developed over the centuries, so most of us have far more rules than we could possibly obey. When we are honest with ourselves, it's clear we sin all the time. Some people have so many rules that the way they get out of bed in the morning could be labeled a sin—I didn't pray first thing. In fact, a sizable chunk of Christianity believes what they call the "total depravity of man." The theory states sin has infected every part of human nature, making humans incapable of knowing or obeying God. It's not your fault, by the way; they blame Adam.

Let's rethink the story of Adam and Eve and see if we can come up with something better to help us understand God. Instead of hiding from God in shame, what do you think would have happened if Adam had stood before God and apologized for what he did? From what I know about God, and remember, I have the advantage of knowing about God from the actions and words of Jesus; I think God would have put his arms around Adam's shoulder, they would have talked it through, and continued with their uninterrupted fellowship. Jesus taught us that God is a forgiving God. Adam did not know that. Jesus explained this concept of a son apologetically returning to a father he had wronged in the parable of the Prodigal Son.

The Adam and Eve story writer didn't know it either because he didn't know Jesus. Eating the fruit was not Adam's sin. It was not knowing God. Neither was taking his inheritance early the prodigal's sin; it was leaving his father's house.

Sin is not a failure of something we do or don't do, in Adam's case, eating the forbidden fruit. Sin is a failure to be something. It's a failure to be what God made us, His companion, communicant (a communicant is a person who receives communion). Humans were made for a relationship, and sin is the result of failing to fulfill that role. God didn't evict Adam from the garden. Adam evicted himself when he hid from God. You can't be in a relationship with God when you're hiding from Him. Adam was ashamed of what he had done and did not want to be with God.

One of the basic tenets of the Christian faith is that humans are estranged from God because of sin. However, because of God's love, Jesus (God's Son) came to tell us that we can reconnect and have fellowship with God. How this happened is disputed, and volumes have been written to explain it. The ultimate result is that many think humans are required to do something before fellowship with God can be enjoyed. The requirement might be as easy as reciting a simple statement of belief, usually called "The Sinner's Prayer," or as complex as obeying a significant set of rules. In a later chapter, we'll discuss religion and how it works.

From the moment of creation, God wanted to live in a relationship with humans. A perfect place was created, and all needs were provided. Despite the frequent communion with God, Adam did not understand God. He had the opinion that God would withhold something good from him, despite everything God had already provided. A relationship with God was not possible because Adam didn't understand God.

When the word *sin* is used in the New Testament, it's often a translation of the Greek word *hamartano*. If you grew up going to church, you probably heard that the word means missing the mark, like an archer missing the bull's eye or the target altogether. It's not that the archer did something mean or evil; he simply missed. Perhaps he was careless, didn't take the wind into account, or didn't practice enough; the bottom line is that he missed.

When Paul said, "for all have sinned and fall short of the glory of God" (Romans 3:23), he didn't mean that we're all evil or immoral. He means that we missed the mark and fell short of the target. In this case, the target is "the glory of God."

If the target is God's glory, we need to understand what that means. When the prophet Isaiah had a vision in the temple, he saw the

Lord sitting on the throne surrounded by angels shouting, "Holy, Holy, Holy is the Lord of armies. The whole earth is full of his glory" (Isaiah 6:3). The Hebrew language implies glory means weight or wealth. Taken together, it suggests a wealthy person who carries much weight, heavy with money.

When applied to God, obviously, God is not wealthy in terms of money but does have an abundance of weighty positive attributes. When we speak of God's glory, it is a reference to the character and qualities of God. We think of terms like majesty, opulence, splendor, and magnificence. But what (Who) is the clearest manifestation of God? Where do we see the purest expression of God's glory? The answer is simple—Jesus. To sin and fall short of God's glory means we missed the mark established by Jesus. Jesus revealed God's glory as kindness, gentleness, goodness, love, self-sacrificing. When we are not like Jesus, it is sin. The Westminster Confession reminds us that "the chief end of man is to glorify God." It is our primary vocation.

From the beginning, man is identified as being made in the "image of God" (Genesis 1:26). This truth is repeated several times. In 1 Corinthians 11, Paul identifies man as "the image and glory of God."

Returning to Paul's word in Romans 3, we fall short of God's glory because of sin. It wasn't 24 sins that caused Adam problems; it was one sin of failing to know God. Specifically, it was missing the mark of being the image and glory of God. Sin is not being what God made us. Adam's sin (remember, he represents all humans) was missing the target. He was not thrown out of the Garden by an angry God; he wandered away from a loving God that he misunderstood.

Several years ago, my wife's grandmother lived with us for a while. She had a Pentecostal background and was accustomed to expressing emotion when feeling especially close to God. On more than one occasion, Grandma would shout the word "glory" out of the blue. It was precipitated by seeing something that reminded her of God's goodness or perhaps a memory of something God had done. The only thing she knew to do at such times was to declare God's glory.

That's what happens with people who live in a relationship with God. I don't mean we should go around shouting "glory" all the time. But we will be aware of God's glory because we know him from personal experience. That is our chief purpose in life. That is how we fellowship with God.

My wife and I have been married for nearly 48 years. We knew each other as friends for three or four years before that. I'm confident that I know her better than anyone else in the world, better even than her brother or sister, who have known her longer. Yet, no matter how well I know Sharon, occasionally, I do something inconsiderate (that means "without consideration" of what I should have known), and our communion is broken. In other words, we'll both go into the other room and pout a bit. At that point, the most foolish thing I can do is avoid her, run away and hide somewhere.

Yet, that is precisely what Adam did. Despite his knowledge of God, when he did something that he knew was inconsiderate (there's that word again) of God, he hid, and the relationship was broken. Some would say the world has been messed up ever since. However, it's not messed up because of Adam but because "all of us have sinned" (Romans 3:23).

What happened next?

Part 2: God's Desire Enlightened by Tradition

"*Those who don't know* history are destined to repeat it," wrote Spanish philosopher George Santayana. The words were tweaked a little by Winston Churchill and have been repeated countless times since. History is a valuable teacher, although seldom a popular subject in school. The other day, I saw a funny meme that said, "Those who don't know history are doomed to repeat it while the rest of us have to watch."

One of the best sources of information when writing the biography of God is to study history. Since God is not a visible entity, we can't dig up old photos, but we can read the accounts of what God has done throughout history. If I may paraphrase a comment about Jesus by the Apostle John, all the libraries in the world could not contain all the things that have been written about God.

History is filled with the things of God. I'll be the first to admit to skepticism that God truly did all the things credited to him by eager writers, but there is much recorded that does smack of authenticity.

Remember, the thesis of this book is that every contact between God and man is motivated by God's desire for a relationship. History confirms that thesis. Bear in mind also that this is a *brief* history of God, so I'm only going to list the highlights.

Also, keep in mind that my tradition is Christianity. When I speak of history as related to God, I have been steeped in the history recorded in what we call the Old Testament and the New Testament. My tradition is extremely important to my understanding of God. I have been taught the Bible is the record of what God has done in history.

As a kid, a good way to confound a Sunday School teacher was to ask if the pagans in Africa knew about God. I admit, the question was motivated by a desire to distract the teacher rather than a quest for knowledge. Later, I learned those pagans in Africa and numerous other people around the world also had a history with God. It was different than mine, but it was informative and important to them. Judaism, Islam, and Christianity share the same history interpreted differently. Buddhism, Confucianism, and other eastern religions have completely different histories, as does every tribal religion.

All of us have a tradition that informs what we know about God. To write a history of God would be incomplete without considering these traditions. (I'm aware that Karen Armstrong did just that in her New York Times bestseller, *The History of God*, a much longer book.) The next few pages describe the relationship between God and humans as understood by Christians.

The story of Adam is the story of all of us. As we have already noted, Paul reminds us that all have sinned and turned away from God. It didn't take long for Adam (remember, *Adam* stands for *mankind*) to realize things were better off inside the garden than outside. He wanted to find a way to make things right with God. He needed a way to appease God.

Apparently, he devised some type of sacrificial system. Adam's sons, Cain and Abel, offered sacrifices designed to make God happy. It was the beginning of religion. That is essentially the definition of religion. Religion is an attempt to return to a relationship with God. Rituals and rules are developed to make this happen. For ancient man, most religions focused on offering sacrifices that would earn God's favor and blessing.

Religions differ in how this is accomplished. Early humans relied heavily on offering sacrifices. As cultures advanced, physical sacrifices disappeared and morphed into keeping rules, adopting a unique lifestyle, or believing a set of propositions.

We are unable to determine major portions of our lives. For example, we don't decide if we're going to be white, black, or brown. We don't choose the language we are taught as a child. Most of us continue to live in the country where we were born, although more are changing countries now than in the past. I know people who have lived in the same neighborhood their entire life. I've also met people who have barely traveled; some have never been to another state, much less another country.

The same is true for religion. Most people stick with the same religion they were taught as a child. I'm not talking about a Baptist who becomes a Lutheran because their spouse insists. I mean, Christians stay Christians, Muslims stay Muslims, Buddhists stay Buddhists, etc. The truth is that many of us don't even consider the possibility. We might not be a very good Christian, but we're convinced it's the only valid religion.

Not only do we give little or no thought to any other religion, but we also fail to understand the origin of religion, not just our chosen religion, but the idea of religion itself. God did not create religions. They are developed by humans (almost exclusively men, not women) as a way to achieve safety from divine wrath and secure divine assistance. Adopting a religion is like hiring an alarm company to keep watch over your house and all your stuff. We want to feel safe, free from worry or concern about what might happen.

Estimates suggest there are 10,000 religions in the world, although more than 80% of the people practice some form of Christianity, Islam, Buddhism, or Hinduism. Few people go through life without some form of religion.

The purpose of religion is to inform how to relate to God. The principles discussed apply to all religions, but I will use the Christian religion specifically since I know it the best from experience. Once humans determined there was a God who exerted some type of control over the world; it became imperative to discover how to stay on God's good side. After all, if God holds the power to create, then he must also have the power to destroy. Therefore, the two common threads running through all religions are worship and obedience.

The need to know how to please or appease God is because life goes on after death. No major religion teaches that existence ends at death. Eternal life is understood in a variety of ways described by the chart:

Christianity:
- Heaven/Hell
- Salvation from sin necessary
- Get to heaven by faith in Jesus

Islam
- Heaven/Hell
- Salvation from sin not necessary
- Get to heaven by good works

Buddhism
- Reincarnation
- Salvation from sin not necessary
- Achieve Nirvana through Meditation and other practices

Judaism
- Heaven/Hell
- Salvation by offeirng sacrifices
- Get to heaven by sacrifices and obedience

God is worshipped because God is God, and we are not. Religions develop worship styles so adherents can acknowledge this difference. For many religions, worship involves singing, dancing, chanting, or other visible manifestations. For others, worship occurs in the quiet solitude of meditation. Worship often includes some type of offering. It might be as simple as water, fruit, flowers, or incense. For Muslims, praying and reading sacred writings constitute worship. For Buddhists, it is sitting and chanting.

Christian worship involves singing, choral or individual, ecstatic utterances (Pentecostals), offerings, and prayer. The purpose is to declare the greatness of God and express adoration of God and gratitude for God's gifts. Christians are expected to worship frequently, although it's not required, as we will see in a few moments. Christian offerings consist of money or time.

Religion tells us what we must do in order to be safe. In fact, Christianity actually uses the word *saved*. Christians frequently talk about being saved. What is meant by that is there is something we can do to ensure we are good with God. We can be safe from any kind of eternal punishment.

The Christian religion teaches that faith in Jesus guarantees this freedom. Christians differ on what this means. Most Catholics define a threefold faith. First, it's more than intellectual acceptance of church doctrine. It requires trusting God to the point of accepting his plan for our life and rejecting our selfish will and ways. The second element is commitment to service and acts of charity motivated by loving God and others. The third element is the sacraments. The Catholic Church has several sacraments, but Baptism and the Eucharist are required.

Worldwide, the Catholic Church represents the largest number of Christians. The second largest group is Evangelicals. We hear a great deal about Evangelicals in the United States because they have crossed over and become a political party. The Evangelical view of salvation also involves faith in Jesus. The biggest difference from Catholics is that faith begins with a one-time experience. Salvation is the result of deliberately declaring faith in Jesus.

Evangelicals have made this easier by condensing it to a simple process. It is frequently called the "Sinner's Prayer." The precise words don't matter, but it typically goes like this: "Dear God, I confess I'm a sinner. I believe Jesus died for my sins. By faith, I accept His gift and place my faith in him. Amen."

Some Evangelicals believe that once you say this prayer, you're good for all time—once saved, always saved, is what they say. Others believe it's not necessarily permanent but can be lost, either by neglect or denial.

What It Means to be "Safe"

Since most humans believe that life continues after death, either through reincarnation or transitioning to an eternal place (think heaven or hell), the issue becomes how do we guarantee that we get to the right destination. After all, we don't want to board the wrong plane and end up in Atlanta instead of Chicago (you can decide which city represents hell).

The predominant premise of Christianity is that sin causes humans to be estranged from God. Growing up in the Christian faith, I frequently heard how sin separates us from God. We have a sin problem that must be resolved before we can be in a relationship with God and be *safe* for eternity.

A major early flaw of Christianity was to absorb Judaism. Jesus lived in a Jewish community, and Paul was raised as a Jew and became a murderous advocate of the doctrine. However, Jesus frequently offered himself to Gentiles (non-Jews) and continually clashed with Jewish leaders about the necessity of Jewish practices. Paul also spoke repeatedly about God's love for the Gentiles as much as the Jews (see Romans).

Several times in the Sermon on the Mount (Matthew 4-6), Jesus said, "You have heard..." in reference to Jewish practice, "but I say..." offering a different interpretation. In the Gospel of John, we are reminded over and over that Jesus came for the whole world. The first verse that many of us memorized as kids was John 3:16 – "For God so loved the world that he gave his only begotten son that all who believe in him might be saved." Jesus came to benefit the entire world, all of humanity. Paul says specifically God is not the God of the Jews only but also the Gentiles (Romans 3:29).

For a long time, Christians have lived as if it's necessary to become a Jew before becoming a Christian. They never come out and say it, but they have adopted Jewish thinking in most of what they do.

Years ago, when I was a young pastor, an older Deacon in our church had to have surgery. He was embarrassed, but I visited him in the hospital because that's what pastors did in those days. He was in his 60s, but he had to be circumcised. Sitting next to his bed, I assured him that after his surgery, he was now safe both ways. He had been baptized and circumcised; he was covered, fully insured.

I was joking because Christians didn't adopt the requirement of circumcision. However, they did adopt the Jewish sacrificial system.

As already noted, a common feature found in the religion of early human tribes was offering sacrifices. It made sense that the best way to earn God's favor was to give him an offering. Since God had to eat (remember, humans have typically pictured a God who looks much like us), the best thing to sacrifice to him was food—fruit, vegetables, and especially meat. Offering an entire animal was a great sacrifice that would certainly please God. Sacrifices appear very early in the first chapters of Genesis when Cain and Abel offered sacrifices to God. There is no indication that God asked for a sacrifice.

For some reason, we have no idea why one offering was acceptable, and the other was not. As a result, Cain was angry and eventually killed his brother. If you want a suggestion on why Abel's offering was acceptable and Cain's not, pick a Bible commentator, and you'll get a different one for each writer you choose. It doesn't matter. We don't have any reason to believe that God wanted/needed any kind of offering. The sacrificial system was not God's creation. It was an invention by humans to try and win God's favor.

The sacrificial system became a central part of Israel's religion. The book of Leviticus spells out numerous types of offerings designed for various purposes. Israel's faith was built around giving offerings to God, culminating with the construction of the temple in Jerusalem, designed uniquely to bring humans and God together via sacrifices. It was Israel's way to live in a relationship with God.

A problem arose in 70 A.D. when the Romans destroyed the Temple, which was necessary for offering sacrifices. The Temple has never been rebuilt, yet Judaism continues to exist. What they did was internalize the sacrifices, and they evolved into prayers and actions of repentance, forgiveness, and atonement. Since they were no longer physically able to do what was necessary to be forgiven and accepted by God, they came up with a different solution.

Christianity came along and adopted the basic premise behind Israel's concept of God needing a sacrifice. After the final Old Testament prophet Malachi, it took 400 years for another prophet to appear out in the wilderness. John the Baptizer identified Jesus as the Lamb of God. Many Christians have taken that to mean that God was offering Jesus as the ultimate, final sacrifice necessary to please God.

It's clear from what is said throughout the New Testament that Jesus died (shed blood) to radically change things. However, his death was not to appease God or satisfy a need for punishment of sin. What we learn from Jesus is that "instead of us needing to spill blood to get to God, we have God spilling blood to get to us!" (see Richard Rohr).

Most ancient religions pictured God eating humans, animals, and crops that were sacrificed to him on altars. Jesus came along with a message that turned this upside down. This radical approach is most clearly reflected in what Christians call *The Last Supper* or *Eucharist*. Hours before his death, Jesus gathered his disciples in a room to share a meal. During the supper, Jesus took the bread, broke it, and distributed it around the room saying, "This is My body, which is being given for you..." (Luke 22:19). Then he took a cup of wine and shared it with the words, "This cup, which is poured out for you, is the new covenant in My blood" (Luke 22:20). God wanted communion so much that he brought the food for them to share.

God didn't need a sacrifice or any kind of offering to welcome humans. Jesus wasn't provided as a payment by God to himself. Yet, because the church swallowed the religion of Judaism, they had to find a way to fulfill God's need for a sacrifice, and Jesus fit that purpose. Christian history is replete with attempts to explain the meaning of Jesus' death. Theologians call it the Doctrine of Atonement, and they provide theories about how God and humans got together. The New Testament has many references to Jesus' death on the cross being the decisive moment in history that united us with God.

Jesus' death was definitely a sacrifice, but it wasn't because God required one. He tried repeatedly to tell Israel that He did not want their sacrifices. Listen to the words of the Prophets:

"Go, learn the meaning of the words, what I want is mercy, not sacrifice, knowledge of God, not burnt offerings in the temple." (Hosea 6:6)

This is what the Lord of armies, the God of Israel says: "Add your burnt offerings to your sacrifices and eat flesh. For I did not speak to your fathers, or command them on the day that I brought them out of the land of Egypt, concerning burnt offerings and sacrifices. But this is what I commanded them, saying, 'Obey My voice, and I will be your God, and you will be My people; and you shall walk entirely in the way which I command you, so that it may go well for you.'" (Jeremiah 7: 21-23)

Jeremiah said it as clearly as possible. God did not command them to bring burnt offerings and sacrifices. He wanted them to hear His voice and be His people. Sadly, Israel paid more attention to their neighbors and developed an elaborate system of sacrifices and offerings, and completely missed what God wanted. In his prayer of repentance, the Psalmist was aware of this truth:

For You do not delight in sacrifice, otherwise I would give it;
You do not take pleasure in burnt offering.
The sacrifices of God are a broken spirit;
A broken and a contrite heart, God, You will not despise. (Psalm 51:16-17)

"You do not want sacrifices and offerings;
You do not ask for animals burned whole on the altar or for sacrifices to take away sins."
Instead, David wrote: "You have given me ears to hear you, and so I answered, 'Here I am; your instructions for me are in the book of the Law.'" (Psalm 40:6-7 The Good News Bible)

The writer of Hebrews, who was obviously well-versed in the theology and inner workings of Israel's sacrificial system, echoed these same truths:

For it is impossible for the blood of bulls and goats to take away sins. (Hebrews 10:4)

For this reason, when Christ was about to come into the world, he said to God:
"You do not want sacrifices and offerings,
But you have prepared a body for me.
You are not pleased with animals burned whole on the altar
or with sacrifices to take away sins.
Then I said, 'Here I am to do your will, O God,
Just as it is written of me in the book of the Law.'" (Hebrews 10:5-7 The Good News Bible)

The earliest church fathers, the ones closest to the New Testament era, expressed what has become known as the Moral Example Theory. Augustine, writing in the 5th century, taught that Jesus lived and died to bring about a positive change through his teaching and actions. He is our example to follow. His death was important because it inspired people to live good, moral lives. The focus is as much on Jesus' life as his death (see Romans 5:10-11).

The Ransom Theory posits that Jesus died as a ransom, paid either to Satan or God, to free humans from bondage (see Mark 10:45). His death was a payment to satisfy the debt inherited from Adam's original sin. In a similar vein, the Christus Victor theory is slightly different. Jesus didn't ransom humans from Satan. He simply defeated evil, like Liam Neeson, freeing his daughter from human traffickers in the movie *Taken*. Jesus won the victory due to his sinless life (see Romans 5:12-21).

In response to the Ransom Theory, Anselm developed the Satisfaction Theory. It didn't seem feasible that God owed anything to Satan, so Jesus was not paying a ransom. Instead, Jesus died to satisfy the justice of God. It's called the Satisfaction Theory. Once God was satisfied with Jesus' death, the relationship between God and humans was repaired (see Hebrews 10:11-14).

The most popular theory proposed by Luther and the reformers was a refinement of the Satisfaction Theory. Jesus died to satisfy God's wrath against sin. He was punished. That's why it's called "Penal Substitution Theory." The punishment was necessary to satisfy the justice of God and the legal demand that God punish sin. Consequently, now that sin has been punished, God can forgive sinners. God needed to punish sin, and something happened with Jesus on the cross that was sufficient (see 2 Corinthians 5:21; Galatians 3:13).

Writing about the various theories surrounding the need for Jesus' death, C.S. Lewis explained it in "Mere Christianity." "Now before I became a Christian I was under the impression that the first thing Christians had to believe was one particular theory as to what the point of this dying was. According to that theory God wanted to punish men for having deserted and joined the Great Rebel, but Christ volunteered to be punished instead, and so God let us off. Now I admit that even this theory does not seem to me quite so immoral and so silly as it used to, but that is not the point I want to make. What I came to see later on was that neither this theory nor any other is Christianity. The central Christian belief is that Christ's death has somehow put us right with God and given us a fresh start. Theories as to how it did this are another matter. A good many different theories have been held as to how it works; what all Christians are agreed on is that it does work. I will tell you what I think it is like. All sensible people know that if you are tired and hungry a meal will do you good. But the modern theory of nourishment—all about the vitamins and proteins—is a different thing. People ate their dinners and felt better long before the theory of vitamins was ever heard of: and if the theory of vitamins is some day abandoned they will go on eating their dinners just the same. Theories about Christ's death are not Christianity: they are explanations about how it works. Christians would not all agree as to how important those theories are."

All of these theories are flawed because they miss the central message of Jesus—violence is not defeated by violence. Yes, Jesus is the *lamb of God* who takes away our sin (see John 1:29), but He is a lamb, not a lion. He transformed the very worst of humanity not by violently destroying God's created animals but by exposing the violence. He became the one suffering from that violence. His message was not to rejoice in the violence but to turn the other cheek.

Hanging on the cross, Jesus was not changing God's mind about humans. He was changing our minds about God. Stop the violence and killing. That's not of God or what God wants. The solution to our sin problem is to follow Jesus, transforming our violent world by love and suffering with those who suffer.

Do We Need to Earn God's Favor?

I've written many pages so far, and I hope there is one thing that comes out repeatedly—God wants to live in a relationship with humans. That is why we are here as well as the motive behind everything God has done in the world. Adam's sin did not diminish God's desire for us, and neither did your sin. All that needs to happen is that we return to God.

Earlier I referred to Jesus' story of the Prodigal Son. That story clearly spells out the relationship between God and humans. The younger son wanted to leave his father's house and make his own way in the world. The boy didn't commit some atrocious sin that offended his father. He didn't trample on the rose bushes in the garden when he left home. He simply took his inheritance, freely given by the father, and set out to make his mark in the world.

We don't know how long it took, but the boy burned his way through the inheritance and found himself feeding hogs, hoping for a share of their feed. Deciding to return to his father where he knew things were better, the boy set off for home. Along the way, he thought seriously to come up with the perfect words of sorrow so his father would allow him to live among the servants. He had no hope of getting his room back.

As the young man approached home, he was spotted by his father while still a long way off. This was not an accidental sighting. The father was on the front porch, scanning the horizon in hopes of seeing his son. All he wanted was for his son to come back.

Those who propose various theories of atonement to explain Jesus' death on the cross would have us believe the prodigal boy needed to come home with one of the pigs he was feeding underneath his arm. After all, the father needed to be appeased. Somehow, the boy needed to pay for his disobedience.

But, read Jesus' story carefully. The boy didn't bring a sacrifice. When the father saw the boy coming up the road, he called to his servants and gave them instructions, "Quickly bring out the best robe and put it on him, and put a ring on his finger and sandals on his feet; and bring the fattened calf, slaughter it, and let's eat and celebrate" (Luke 15:22-23). The father, who represents God, provided the calf for slaughter, not as a means of atonement but for celebration.

The returning son had nothing to offer to his father. He squandered everything, even to the point of being on the verge of starvation. However, he did have the only thing the father wanted—a relationship with his son.

If Jesus didn't die because God needed a sacrifice for sinful humans, we are left with the question of why did he die? We'll explain that in a subsequent section.

Since man was created for the purpose of having a relationship, God was not willing to allow this separation to continue, so He acted. Before we examine what God did, I need to make a few comments about the record in the early chapters of Genesis. After the story of creation and Adam exiting the garden, chapter 4 describes Adam's sons and their dispute and genealogy. In chapter 5, we find further genealogical information that stretches the imagination, for example, some guy named Methuselah who lived 969 years.

Genesis 6 begins with the story of corruption and the introduction of Noah. You recall the story. God warned Noah that He was going to destroy the earth but preserve Noah and the animals. Chapters 7-10 provide a detailed account of the flood. We need to think about that for the next few paragraphs.

Ancient people did not have the information we possess today about the weather. If I didn't listen to forecasts, there is little I could tell you about what to expect. One of the few things I know about the weather is that we have an especially warm day, and the wind is strong from the south; it's probably going to be colder tomorrow. I have no idea why but that's what I have observed. Without modern technology and reporting, I would probably be like people of old and credit God with what happens.

Perhaps a modern analogy might help explain this concept. Let's say that I have a great job. I prayed for a job just like this, and it is precisely what I need and want. After a few years of working, I get a new boss. For some reason, the new boss doesn't like me (I think he wants to give my job to a cousin). One day the boss tells me that he wants to meet with me on Friday afternoon. I know I'm about to be fired. What do I do? Among other things, I pray, asking God to take care of this situation.

When I show up for work on Friday, the office is buzzing with news. The new boss had a heart attack the night before and died. Suddenly my job is safe. God answered my prayer. I go home and tell my wife and kids how God provided. The story becomes one of those family legends about how dad's job was spared when God killed his boss. Do I really think God killed my boss? No, because I have heard Jesus and realize that God loves each of us, my unfair boss included. My boss died because he had a bad diet, was overweight, family history, high blood pressure, or whatever, not because God killed him.

However, what if I don't know Jesus? The meaning of the story is the same, but some of the things I thought were real, need to be re-thought. Perhaps that's a good way to examine the story of Noah and the flood. The meaning of the story doesn't need to change, but it will be good to reconsider the details recorded by a writer who didn't know Jesus, so he didn't know as much about God as we do.

Archaeologists have determined that it is likely a great flood covered the Mesopotamian Valley in 2900 B.C. It is the source of several ancient flood stories told by other religions. What that suggests is that there was a flood that perhaps covered and destroyed a good portion of the *known* world. There are no satellite photos to confirm the reality or extent of such a flood.

The Old Testament writers picked up the accounts of this catastrophic event circulating from generation to generation and applied them to what they understood about God. It is crucial to remember at this point that their understanding of God was pre-Jesus, so it was not fully developed. Israel's tradition shaped a story that explained how a tragic event was an example of the greatness of their God. Other ancient civilizations passed on similar stories that made their God the cause.

The story of Noah in Genesis is not history or meteorology. Rather than telling what happened, the story is valuable because it tells us what Israel believed about God. In the same way, the two stories of creation are not a historical account of a primordial paradise; the flood story tells us something valuable. In the creation story, the water was separated from the earth. In the flood story, the water rained down, and creation was returned to chaos. Creation was undone, and there was a new Adam. His name was Noah.

It is crucial to understand once again that Israel did not have the benefit of Jesus to help them understand God. What they knew was that a terrible tragedy happened, and their ancestors survived, so obviously, God did it. He caused the flood. The fact that the flood destroyed everyone not in Noah's family is not the point. They were still like Adam, unaware of God's love, grace, and forgiveness.

The flood provided an opportunity to start over. Back to my Systematic Theology classes, we always studied the characteristics of God. We learned about omnipresence (God is everywhere at all times), omnipotence (God is all-powerful), omniscience (God knows everything), and several other traits. However, I don't remember any reference to God's omnipersistence (God is stubborn).

One of the history lessons is that God does not give up. That's especially good news when it applies to humans; God does not give up on us. We see it over and over again when God is rebuffed but always tries again.

At this point, we need to raise a question that might make some of us uncomfortable. When all of mankind except one turned out to be wicked, is it possible to say that God failed? He went to great lengths and spent an enormous amount of time creating a being that would allow Him to live in community, but it didn't work.

One possible response is that God didn't fail, but man was the failure. However, God created the human and established the parameters that would have allowed him to stay in community with God. Man didn't keep up his end of the bargain, causing them both to fail.

As a lifelong baseball fan, I can attest that one of the rarest things in the sport is what is called a "perfect game." It occurs when one team has zero batters reach first base. The credit is given to the pitcher, and he is always remembered for pitching a perfect game. In more than 150 seasons, there have only been 23 perfect games.

Although the pitcher gets credit when it happens, it's always the team that makes it happen. It seems that in many perfect games, a fielder makes a spectacular play that allows it to happen. There have also been countless games that fell short of perfection, not because of the pitcher but because of a fielder who missed a play or made an error. The pitcher gets no credit for a nearly perfect game.

God is like the pitcher who did his part but was let down by humans. His quest for establishing the perfect world failed. He gets no credit for creating a perfect world because it wasn't.

Noah was not a perfect man in a perfect place like Adam, the first man. He was a good man being righteous in an evil place. Because of Noah, God did not need to start over; He simply spared him from the fate of the flood that awaited everyone else. There has been speculation that Noah spent the time it took to build the Ark, calling people to repent and turn to God. However, the writer of the account in Genesis doesn't say anything about that, and Jesus said the flood came as a surprise. Salvation from the coming flood belonged only to Noah and his family, not to anyone else.

A common thread running through God's history to this point is that each major event was His attempt to live in relationship with a willing human. As we continue to work our way through history, we will notice this desire constantly at the forefront of what God does in the world. If it's that important to God, it probably deserves greater recognition from humans.

I'm going to take a personal side step and address another issue. Many Christians do not understand that God is striving to have a personal relationship with humans. It's the reason for creation and the motivation behind God's actions since. Yet, many hold the opinion that God's desire is to save us from death and hell. Their only goal is to acquire what they call eternal life, and once that's secured, little else matters. Even though many understand God's desire for fellowship, they plan on that happening in heaven, don't worry about it now.

As we will see while continuing our way through God's history, He is intent on fellowship now, not something in the future. He has done much to make it happen. If it's that important to him, it should be equally important to us.

Part 3: God's Desire Explained in Jesus

Even though I already included a quote from C.S. Lewis that is required in all published Christian books, here is another that is equally appropriate:

"I am trying here to prevent anyone saying the really foolish thing that people often say about Him [that is, Christ]: 'I'm ready to accept Jesus as a great moral teacher, but I don't accept His claim to be God.' That is the one thing we must not say. A man who was merely a man and said the sort of things Jesus said would not be a great moral teacher. He would either be a lunatic–on a level with the man who says he is a poached egg–or else he would be the Devil of Hell. You must make your choice. Either this man was, and is, the Son of God: or else a madman or something worse.... You can shut Him up for a fool, you can spit at Him and kill Him as a demon; or you can fall at His feet and call Him Lord and God. But let us not come up with any patronising nonsense about His being a great human teacher. He has not left that open to us. He did not intend to." –C.S. Lewis in Mere Christianity

Who was Jesus?

That is probably the most important question ever asked. It has been debated and dissected for 2,000 years. There is little disagreement that Jesus was a Jewish man who lived in Israel in the early part of the first century. He is the baseline for calendars, the zenith for ethicists, and the object of worship for a good portion of humans.

Jesus is recognized as special by several major religions. Christians identify him as the Son of God. Buddhists claim that he reached a high state of an enlightened person. For the Hindus, Jesus preached the same message as Lord Krishna. The Muslim Quran speaks of Jesus' virgin birth, his miracles, and ascension to heaven. No other individual has ever been held in such high regard by so many.

Who was Jesus?

The question has been around since before Jesus died. Walking with his disciples one day, Jesus asked them, "Who do people say that I am?" (Mark 8:27).

Their reply suggested the talk of the day was that he was either John the Baptist, Elijah or another prophet. Then Jesus specifically asked his followers, "But who do you say that I am?"

Peter spoke up and said, "You are the Christ" (Mark 8:29).

Apparently, Peter hit the mark because Jesus "warned them to tell no one about him." It wasn't time for the world to know his identity.

God Among Us

If Peter was correct, as Jesus intimated, then the real question is, "what does it mean to be the Christ?"

In his book, *The Universal Christ*, Richard Rohr has a chapter titled "Christ Is Not Jesus's Last Name." We tend to use the names *Jesus* and *Christ* interchangeably, like you can call me *William* or *Terry*. However, for Jesus, they have different meanings and represent different truths.

In Jesus' birth story, Mary was instructed to give him the name Jesus. The name identified him for the 33 years he walked the roads of Judea and Galilee. It appears to be a new name as it does not occur in the Old Testament. According to Isaiah's prophecy, the name was to be Immanuel (see Isaiah 7:14). He was called *Jesus* like I'm called *Terry*, or you're called *Freddy* (or whatever).

Jesus was also identified as *Christ*. You've seen the word translated as *Messiah* and also as *Christ*. It comes from the word for *anoint*, which means to smear oil or any other substance on something. It is a means of designating a person with honor or prestige. In this case, it is God who anoints, so it refers to the one identified as God's chosen, or in the case of Jesus Christ, God himself. Christ is God in the same way Jesus is God.

One of the clearest expressions of Christ is found in the first chapter of John's Gospel. In the first 18 verses, we learn these qualities of Christ:

- **Eternal** (vs.1-3) – Christ has no beginning and no end.
- **Creator** (v.3) – Christ was the agent of creation prior to any type of Big Bang and certainly before Adam and Eve frolicked in the garden.
- **Light and Life** (vs.4-5) – Christ is the source of life. To be light means that Christ illuminates everything. Later, John describes the improper and proper responses to light (see John 3:19-21).
- **Incarnate** (v.14) – Christ became flesh and lived among us on the earth.

The inescapable conclusion is that Christ and Jesus are the same. Jesus is Christ, and Christ is Jesus. Everything that Christ is, Jesus is, and everything Jesus is, Christ is. Christ is the way to express God in tangible form. Remember, God is spirit, not observable or knowable to humans. When God wanted to reveal Himself, He did it through Christ. Christ is the tangible God. Christ is the form of God perceived by one of our senses.

Earlier, we spoke of God's revelation. What that means is that he made himself perceivable. When you see God, you're actually seeing Christ (see Romans 1:20). The natural world is an expression of the creator and, as Paul intimates, clear enough to allow humans to understand God. It might be correct to say that creation was the first incarnation and Jesus was the second. In creation, God was visible in the natural world. In Jesus, God was visible in a man.

Paul gave his life to prove that Jesus is the Christ (Acts 9:22). He uses the phrase "in Christ" 164 times. This suggests it is his term for being a Christian (remember, *Christian* is not what early believers called each other). The term "Christ" comes from a verb meaning "to anoint." It has the same background and meaning as the word "Messiah," the Hebrew expression of God's savior.

Matthew uses the term Messiah five times. Matthew wrote with the intention of proving Jesus was the King ushering in a new Kingdom.

John used the term twice, once on the lips of Andrew when he called his brother Peter by saying, "We have found the Messiah." The other time was a statement by the woman at the well who did not yet recognize that Jesus was the Messiah. In his Pentecost sermon, Peter came out and said, "God has made him both Lord and Christ—this Jesus whom you crucified" (Acts 2:36). At least 3,000 believed it that day.

There is a handful of traits possessed by God that nearly every Christian would agree:

- God is eternal, without beginning or end
- God is creator of the universe
- God is love

Jesus also possesses traits that Christians accept:

- Jesus is eternal, without beginning or end
- Jesus is creator, sustainer of the universe
- Jesus is love

The Apostle Paul describes Christ:

For He rescued us from the domain of darkness, and transferred us to the kingdom of His beloved Son, in whom we have redemption, the forgiveness of sins. He is the image of the invisible God, the firstborn of all creation: for by Him all things were created, both in the heavens and on earth, visible and invisible, whether thrones, or dominions, or rulers, or authorities—all things have been created through Him and for Him. He is before all things, and in Him all things hold together. He is also the head of the body, the church; and He is the beginning, the firstborn from the dead, so that He Himself will come to have first place in everything. For it was the Father's good pleasure for all the fullness to dwell in Him, and through Him to reconcile all things to Himself, whether things on earth or things in heaven, having made peace through the blood of His cross. (Colossians 3:13-20)

Christ is the visible aspect of God seen in everything in the created universe. Jesus Christ is the manifestation of God in human form.

Jesus appeared as a human to give us definitive proof of what God is like and how God wants to have a relationship with all humans.

What Jesus Said to Reveal His Identity

Jesus' prayer for his disciples, recorded in John 17, is filled with statements about his identity. He identified himself as God's son (v.1), he has authority over all mankind (v.2), sent by God (v.3), and he had God's glory before the world existed (v.5). He continued by describing his work as God's work (vs.6-9). Then in verse 10, Jesus said, "... all things that are Mine are Yours, and Yours are Mine...." Finally, he speaks about it being time to leave the world by announcing, "I am coming to You."

The Apostle Paul clarified Jesus' identity when he wrote, "For it was the Father's good pleasure for all the fullness to dwell in Him, and through Him to reconcile all things to Himself, whether things on earth or things in heaven, having made peace through the blood of His cross" (Colossians 1:19-20).

With this understanding of Jesus, we can now consider what Jesus tells us about God. After his baptism and wilderness temptations, he began his public ministry with these words, "Repent, for the kingdom of heaven is at hand" (Matthew 4:17). It's important to note two things in the opening statement to Jesus' public life. First is the call to *repent*. The first thing that comes to mind when thinking of repentance is that we need to stop sinning. Many of us grew up hearing the phrase "repentant sinner."

However, the word *repent* has nothing to do with sinning. It means to change your mind, or more specifically, change your way of thinking. The first thing Jesus said when He began His work was to tell people to change the way they think. He said, "You've been looking at this all wrong, and I've come to help you think about it correctly."

The second thing to note is that a new kind of thinking is necessary because the "kingdom of heaven is at hand." The Jews at that time were looking for God to send the Messiah and establish an earthly kingdom, an enhanced, physical kingdom like David and Solomon. Jesus wasn't bringing an earthly kingdom. His kingdom was far more extensive, including all the heavens. The new way of thinking made living in a new kingdom possible.

This is certainly not the book to dissect all the teaching of Jesus. After all, the title is *A **Brief** History of God*, with emphasis on brief. Let me distill it down to three qualities of God that Jesus emphasized. Our thinking needs to change in these areas.

God's Attitude About Humans

Much of our theology begins with the mistaken notion that God is angry toward humans. This reasoning begins with Adam in the garden. When he sinned, that sin was passed on to his ancestors, which, of course, is every person. Therefore, we are all born sinners. Much like I was born left-handed, and with blue eyes, I was also born as a sinner. In other words, before even nursing once at a mother's breast, a baby is already marked out for God's anger and punishment.

With this understanding of inherited sin, something interesting developed among Christians. Even though that baby who was yet to nurse her mother's milk was born a sinner, we can't fathom the notion that God would condemn such an innocent one, so the concept of "age of accountability" was developed to give children time enough to mature. This was a means to protect God from punishing babies.

The theology behind the idea of an age of accountability is that somehow time is suspended in a child's life, allowing them to do anything without guilt. After all, they are not old enough to understand sin, so there is no need to be forgiven. It's like our legal system that allows people to plead innocent because they are mentally incompetent and unable to understand right and wrong. This concept is necessary if God intends on punishing sinners and every individual is born a sinner. There is no magic age when a child is held accountable as it varies from child to child.

This idea of being born as sinners led to the development of the theory that Jesus' death somehow appeased God's need for justice. We are sinners. A just God needs to punish sin. Jesus took our punishment upon himself.

The idea of an offended God seeking to punish offenders is a common theme throughout the Old Testament and was the dominant thinking when Jesus showed up in the first century. Israel frequently identified God as the cause every time their enemies suffered. God was vigilant in seeking out sinners to punish, and because every human was born a sinner, the hunting was good.

That sounds blunt, but God was not accused of being angry. He was just being just. Sin had to be punished, or God would not be perfect. If God ever accepted sin, he would cease to be God. As long as sin was in the world, someone had to pay.

Three words summarize what Jesus taught about God's attitude toward humans:

Forgiveness

One of Jesus' primary messages was that humans need to change their mind about God and sin. Jesus introduced a new quality possessed by God that had eluded humans for centuries. The concept of forgiveness was seldom addressed in the Old Testament. Even one of the most well-known Psalms acknowledging guilt for sin, the Psalmist claims he was born a sinner as he pleads for mercy (see Psalm 51). Note how the Psalm concludes with reference to God's delight in burnt offerings. The purpose of burnt offerings was to secure atonement, a way to satisfy a God who had to punish something/someone for sin. After pleading for compassion and mercy, he felt a sacrifice was still required.

(I realize that earlier I said the writer of Psalm 51 was aware that God does not *delight* in sacrifices. Yet, for some reason, at the end of the Psalm, he adds, "Then you will delight in righteous sacrifices." Apparently, he is of the opinion there is such a thing as a "righteous sacrifice" that pleases God. However, if the one offering is already righteous, why is a sacrifice needed? It's the same kind of contradiction that Christians encounter when trying to explain why we should live a certain way after all of our sins, past and future, have been forgiven.)

When Jesus showed up, the practice of sacrifices for sin was in full bloom. He came to reveal the truth about God that had been missed.

God is forgiving. Earlier, I made the observation that things might have been much different for Adam if he had confessed his sin and sought forgiveness instead of hiding from God. From what Jesus tells us about God, Adam would have been forgiven and perhaps, allowed to remain in the Garden. I don't know how God would have responded, but Jesus doesn't talk about the justice of God. However, he does talk about the forgiveness of God. In fact, God's forgiveness is behind everything Jesus was and said.

Jesus called us to be merciful, just like our father in heaven (Luke 6:36). In the parable known as the *Pharisee and the Tax Collector*, Jesus contrasted the self-righteous prayer of a Pharisee with the prayer of a humble tax collector. Beating his chest, the tax collector said, "God, have mercy on me, a sinner" (Luke 6:13). Jesus added the point of the story is that the man went home justified before God; no sacrifice was offered.

In the Model Pray, Jesus taught us to ask for forgiveness (Matthew 6:14). When the paralyzed man was lowered through the roof to Jesus, instead of declaring the man healed, Jesus forgave his sins. He did it in order to demonstrate his authority to forgive sins (Matthew 9:6). Even while hanging on the cross, Jesus looked down on the insult hurling crowd and soldiers gambling for his garments, and said, "Father, forgive them, for they do not know what they are doing" (Luke 23:34).

Mercy

The dictionary definition of *mercy* is compassion or forgiveness by someone who has the power to punish. This certainly fits God. We can't dispute that God has the power to punish. As Cliff Huxtable used to say to his kids, "I brought you into this world; I can take you out." We need mercy. We can't survive without God's mercy.

After He cast the legion of demons out of the deranged man, Jesus sent him away and instructed him to tell your people, "How much the Lord has done for you, and how he has had mercy on you" (Mark 9:15). When people approached Jesus with a need, they often pled for mercy (the blind man - Mark 10:47; the Canaanite woman with a suffering daughter – Matthew 15:22; father of a son with seizures – Matthew 17:15).

The Jews should have been aware of this quality of God. Mercy is prevalent on the pages of their scriptures (our Old Testament). Psalm 118 reveals God's mercy (lovingkindness, love, in various translations) was a refrain used repeatedly in praise. Israel experienced God's mercy often in its long history. God's mercy is frequently called on when people find themselves in trouble.

Although humans repeatedly appealed to God for mercy, apparently, they did not expect it to happen. Jesus came along with a message to repent, change your thinking about God. God is merciful and expects us to be merciful to one another. He provided a great parable of the king who settled accounts (Matthew 18). A slave who owed a huge amount, far beyond what could ever be repaid, was brought to the king. The man pleaded for patience, and he would repay. Jesus said the king "felt compassion...released him, and forgave him the debt."

The slave turned around and found a man who owed him a much smaller, reasonable debt. Using the exact same language, the man pleaded for patience, and he would repay. By the way, a much more reasonable promise since his debt was much smaller. Instead of forgiving as he had been forgiven, he threw the man in prison until the debt was repaid. When the king heard, he called the slave back and scolded him, "You wicked slave, I forgave you all that debt because you pleaded with me. Should you not also have had mercy on your fellow slave, in the same way that I had mercy on you?" (vs.33-34). Not only is God merciful, but He also expects mercy from each of us.

Grace

A third term that summarizes what Jesus taught about God is *grace*. The simplest, most precise definition of grace is God's favor. God looks upon humans with favor. In the opening words of John's Gospel, Jesus, son of the father, is described as "full of grace and truth" (John 1:14). Interestingly, the word only appears three times in the gospels, all in the first chapter of John. Jesus never uses the word, but he demonstrated the reality because he was "full of grace."

As he traveled through towns and villages proclaiming the kingdom of God and healing multitudes, when he saw the large crowds, "he felt compassion for them, because they were distressed and downcast, like sheep without a shepherd" (Matthew 9:36). When the crowd followed him in the wilderness, after three days, they were hungry, so Jesus miraculously fed them (Matthew 15). When he came upon a funeral and saw a widow grieving the loss of her only son, her only source of provision, he stopped the procession and brought the boy back to life.

Jesus' life was an expression of grace. His presence on the planet proves that God is full of grace toward humans. God did not give up when Adam sinned. He did not quit when Israel refused to go into the promised land. He did not throw up his hands when his people lived in rebellion for centuries. Instead, he sent his best, his only son, as an expression of grace. Listen to how the Apostle Paul describes it: "He predestined us to adoption as sons and daughters through Jesus Christ to Himself, according to the good pleasure of His will, to the praise of the glory of His grace, with which He favored us in the Beloved. In Him we have redemption through His blood, the forgiveness of our wrongdoings, according to the riches of His grace" (Ephesians 1:1-7).

The Old Testament seldom speaks of God's grace, only using the word *grace* a handful of times. However, the New Testament uses the word more than 100 times, and it's especially prevalent in Paul's writings. He understood that everything about our lives is a consequence of God's grace or favorable attitude toward us.

When we look at what Jesus showed us about God, it's hard to understand how humans arrived at the notion that God is angry or that he needs to punish sinners. As I indicated at the beginning of this brief study, the one key thing we know about God is His desire to be in a relationship with humans, and he has worked since the beginning of time to make it happen. Many need to change their thinking (repent) about their understanding of God.

God's Acceptance of Humans

Another flaw in human thinking that needed the truth explained by Jesus was that God is not tribal. Tribal refers to the practice of humans gathering in groups with others of similar ancestry, traditions, or customs. All of us are very tribal. We are most comfortable with those like us. The consequence of surrounding ourselves with "our people" is the conviction those in our group are better than others. We are the ones who are correct while everyone else is wrong.

Jesus made it clear that God does not favor one human over another. Our ancestry, culture, race, religion, or nationality does not matter. God seeks a relationship with every person. One of the earliest songs I learned in Sunday School was *Jesus loves the little children, all the children of the world.*

Gentiles

Jesus lived among the Jews who were convinced they had the scripture to prove they were divinely chosen people. If anyone desired to know and relate to God, it was necessary to become a Jew. God was not interested or concerned with anyone who wasn't a descendant of Abraham.

Jesus came with a new message—God is not tribal.

As he walked down the streets of Capernaum, a Roman Centurion approached Jesus with a request to heal his paralyzed servant. The soldier declared upfront that he was not worthy of Jesus' help but needed it desperately. Jesus responded to his faith and immediately healed his servant.

It took some time for the followers of Jesus to learn this lesson because it was so ingrained in them. After Jesus' death, a Gentile sent word to Peter, wanting to hear the Gospel. Peter fell into a trance and saw a vision that made it clear, Jesus was available to all (see Acts 10). Standing before a room filled with Gentiles, the first words out of his mouth were, "I most certainly understand now that God is not one to show partiality" (Acts 10:34). In the Book of Romans, Paul goes to great lengths to argue that all have the same opportunity with God. He also declared that there is no distinction *in Christ* between Jews or

Greeks, slaves or free, male or female (see I Corinthians 10:32; 12:13; Galatians 3:28).

People needed to learn they did not need to become Jews in order to follow Christ. Jesus told us that God loves every person. There is no need to become something else before God loves us. By the way, many today need to be reminded that God does not love Americans any more than anyone else. Heritage does not provide a special place in God's heart.

Women

First-century Jews (and many 21st century Christians) hold the opinion that women are not on equal footing with men. Jesus lived in a community where women were considered property. They had no rights or opportunities. They lived at the mercy of the men in their lives. They were in dire straits if they didn't have a husband, father, or brother to provide for them. Women were not allowed to worship God fully.

One of the more scandalous things Jesus did occurred with a woman, not just a woman, a Samaritan woman. Not only a female but also a foreigner. He stopped to rest at a well while his disciples went to get food. While alone, the woman came to the well for water, and Jesus asked for a drink. It was not unusual for a man to ask a woman to give him a drink of water, but she was shocked that a Jewish man would ask a Samaritan woman (see John 4). It was shocking. As a result of Jesus' conversation with the woman, many from the village believed in Jesus.

Many of Jesus' most faithful followers were women. It was a woman whose life was changed after being thrown down at Jesus' feet by the judging Pharisees. It was a woman who anointed Jesus' feet and provided an indelible demonstration of real worship. Two women, Mary and Martha, were among Jesus' best friends. It was women who first noticed Jesus had left the grave.

When it comes to God, men have no advantage over women. If women are on an equitable footing with God, then they are also equal in every area of life. Jesus made it clear that God is no respecter of persons.

Religion/Culture/Heritage

The fact that God is not tribal is a direct contrast to humans. We divide ourselves according to religion—Christian, Muslim, Hindu, etc. Even within our religions, we divide ourselves even further into sects or denominations—Catholic, Lutheran, Baptist, etc. It doesn't stop there; you might be Southern, American, Independent, or hundreds of other options as a Baptist. Of course, they are all wrong except ours.

We are also tribal when it comes to nations. We are Americans or French or Chinese, etc., and our country is by far the best. The same is true with our politics, sports teams, hobbies, etc. Humans seek out and gather with their own, and there's nothing wrong with that. It's a good thing. The problem is to think that everyone else is a bad person. If you're not a Baptist, you're going to hell. If you're not an American, you are not as good as us. If you're a Republican, you're an idiot.

This kind of tribalism has been practiced since the beginning of time, each tribe claiming God as their own. Every tribe believes they are on God's side, and everyone else is missing out. Jesus came into that world and showed us that God is on everyone's side; he belongs to everyone's tribe.

One of the most incredible statements in the Bible is, "But now you also, rid yourselves of all of them: anger, wrath, malice, slander, and obscene speech from your mouth. Do not lie to one another, since you stripped off the old self with its evil practices, and have put on the new self, which is being renewed to a true knowledge according to the image of the One who created it— a renewal in which there is no distinction between Greek and Jew, circumcised and uncircumcised, barbarian, Scythian, slave, and free, but Christ is all, and in all" (Colossians 3:8-11). Paul describes how Christ removed the things that divide us and then ends with this amazing statement, "Christ is all, and in all."

We are admonished to eliminate the attitudes and actions that divide us—things like anger, wrath, malice, slander, and obscene speech, and stop lying to one another. The reason is because we all belong to the same tribe, God's tribe. It seems to be human nature to seek out our differences with others, perhaps so we can feel better about ourselves. Our tribes get smaller and smaller because we keep defining more and more people as not belonging.

Christians divide into denominations made up of churches. Churches separate from other churches over theological differences and sometimes political differences. Evangelical Christians don't like Progressive Christians because of their stance on abortion, immigration, giving to the poor, or dozens of other issues. We keep people out of our churches by making it clear what we believe and what behavior is wrong. Look at your tribe. It's possible to be a pro-life, gun-toting, immigrant-hating, gay condemning, Presbyterian (or Baptist, etc.) Christian. It's easy to find other tribe members. Look at the bumper stickers on their car, read their Facebook posts, or find out where they attend church.

Jesus came into that world and said, "Stop! That is not of God."

Humans have failed to heed this message from Jesus concerning God. It is also universally accepted that violence is necessary at times to protect our tribe. I'm not just talking about African or Amazon primitive people fighting neighboring tribes. The worst culprits are the most culturally advanced. How many countries have killed more people than the United States to protect the tribe? I don't know, but if you consider all the wars, even internal wars like the Civil War and the genocide of the Native Americans, I'm not sure any other country would come close. At the same time, we pride ourselves on being the most Christian nation. I'm not sure we can call ourselves Christian when we are so unChristlike (if I'm allowed to create a word).

The primary message of Jesus is that God wants to have a relationship with us, all of us. He is the father, waiting for the prodigal son. Everything God has done was intended to create, continue, and contribute to communion with humans. After each element of creation, God made the observation that it was good. After creating the human, God declared, "it was **very** good." From the beginning, the relationship between God and humans has been special.

If that previous paragraph is true, and of course, I believe it is, then there are serious implications.

God loves every person who ever lived

Many believe that God only cares about the people who follow their particular religion. Unless you're a Christian, God's not interested in you. It's safe to say that most Christians hold this position. Listen to the implications of that position. It means God doesn't care about 70% of the people in the world. I find it impossible to reconcile Jesus' message to that belief. Jesus said, "God so loved the world" (John 3:16). The word translated as "world" is "kosmos" and means the entire universe, including all humans.

God loves the child living in the Asian desert as much as he loves you. He loves the illiterate, uncivilized South American tribal leader as much as you. He loves the atheistic ruler of a Communist country as much as he loves you. He loves the man who has spent his life in the darkest prison as much as he loves you. That doesn't mean God does not love you; it means everyone is loved by God. Jesus came to tell us that and to show us what that means.

God loves the Muslims who kneel several times a day on a prayer rug, the Buddhists sitting with their legs crossed, meditating on life, the African tribe members who gyrate to the numbing beat of drums, and the Christian who kneels at the cross before approaching the altar. God wants to enjoy communion with all of them, and if that is not true for your God, then your God is too small. Jesus called you to repent of that thinking and change your mind.

God is not angry, seeking to punish anyone

We have already discussed the notion that God is angry, seeking to punish sinners. Those who grew up in the church have an image of God being either a loving father or an angry avenger, depending on how humans respond to him. This entire theology of a God of retribution is built on the notion that God is just and cannot tolerate sin.

Consequently, sinners must be punished until they either get right or perish. God is kind of like the American justice system.

Jesus came into a world where people believed God was adamant about punishing sin and sinners. The Pharisees were so intent on avoiding any possibility of experiencing God's anger that they created burdensome rules to keep themselves and others in line. By the way, they were the same people who killed Jesus, not for being a sinner but because Jesus refused to condemn sinners. The people the Pharisees thought would be the recipients of God's anger were the people Jesus ate and partied with.

The way I hear people talking about God, it's easy to understand why people are not interested. When people hear that God sees homosexuals as an abomination, that Muslims are worthy of destruction, and that most people are already doomed for hell, they have no interest in being in a relationship with a God like that.

God is forgiving, seeking to re-establish every broken relationship

I shared a meme recently on Facebook to a page dedicated to discussion about house churches. It's a site with lively discussion on issues broader than church and religion, but usually, the Christian faith comes through. I have no idea who originally made the statement, but the meme reads: "Deconstruction is the revival that evangelicals have been praying for. They just don't have the eyes to see it."

After receiving a few quick "likes," the mood changed. I was attacked for posting "a bunch of Marxist-flavored, destructive, empty, human speculation... The blind leading the blind.... Revival?! Not."

Anyone who follows me on Facebook is well aware that confrontation is not an unusual experience for me. Normally I like confrontation because it can be an opportunity for discussion if the other person is willing. It was not surprising that the concept of deconstruction elicited a negative response. I tried to draw the guy into a productive conversation, but he had a hard time with that.

One advantage of deconstruction can be removing the anger from Christians who want to proclaim the faith. That anger does not work.

It alienates people, turning them off to Jesus. If we can remove the 2,000 years of garbage collected by the church along the way, there will be revival.

Deconstruction is not a new thing. This theme was constant throughout Jesus' time on earth. Many of the metaphors He used expressed this idea of change, finding a new way to think about God and how we relate to God.

Born Again

Nicodemus, a man steeped in the Jews' religion, came to Jesus with a question. It seems that he might have been frightened to ask this question in public, so he came to Jesus "at night." What he was about to ask would have created serious problems if his peers had overheard. Try it yourself; approach your pastor next Sunday morning and ask if it's ok to deconstruct your faith. You will probably get the same kind of reaction that drove Nicodemus into the night.

Nicodemus essentially asked if Jesus was of God. Jesus responded with the familiar words, "unless someone is born again he cannot see the kingdom of God" (John 3:3). Nicodemus thought Jesus was describing some kind of mystical experience of returning to his mother's womb. But, Jesus was not talking about a magical change. Jesus was saying we have to start over from the beginning. We have to be born again, start from the beginning.

Nicodemus, the man immersed in the Jewish religion, said what many Christians have said, "How can these things be?" (John 3:9). He didn't understand, so Jesus referred to Nicodemus' credentials, a "teacher of Israel," the reason you can't understand is because I'm speaking of heavenly things, and you're stuck with earthly thinking.

Nicodemus wanted to find a way to fit Jesus into his religion, but it was not possible. Jesus said you've got to start over. Have you ever thought about what Christianity would be if the church had taken a new approach? Instead of adopting Judaism and making a few changes, what if the church started over with Jesus. (Interesting thoughts for another day.)

When Jesus told a leader of Judaism that he must be born again, essentially, He told the man to deconstruct his faith. In other words, rethink what you believe and practice. John places this encounter at the beginning of his Gospel. From that point forward, Jesus defined what that new faith would look like.

By the way, Paul got it. He said, "...if anyone is in Christ, this person is a new creation; the old things passed away; behold, new things have come" (2 Corinthians 5:17). According to Paul, this new creation occurs because God is in the process of reconciling the world to Himself (v.19). Perhaps the most remarkable statement Paul makes in this passage is that God does not count our wrongdoings against us. Wow. Is Paul saying this new "religion" is not based on the notion that God is out to punish sinners? That's a concept that Nicodemus would never understand without deconstructing.

New Wine into Old Wineskins

The analogies about deconstruction continued with Jesus. Listen to this metaphor: "No one sews a patch of unshrunk cloth on an old garment; otherwise, the patch pulls away from it, the new from the old, and a worse tear results. And no one puts new wine into old wineskins; otherwise the wine will burst the skins, and the wine is lost and the skins as well; but one puts new wine into fresh wineskins" (Mark 2:21-22). We all learned in Sunday School that the old wine sacks would split, and the new wine will be lost.

Jesus brought new wine. It was tempting to make it fit into the old wineskins. The new wine is a new understanding of God. The old wineskin is the religion of the Jews. What Jesus had to say could not be understood by trying to make it fit into Judaism. They tried. The church has tried for 2,000 years. Just one example – Jesus brought the message that God loves all people. The Jews couldn't make it fit because they believed Jews were specially chosen. Christians couldn't make it fit either because all bad people exist outside of God's love. All these years later, many Christians essentially believe that God only loves 30% of the world's population (the number who identify as Christians).

Those who deconstruct are attempting to understand this disconnect. It means to follow the call of Jesus to "rethink."

You Have Been Told...

Five times in the Sermon on the Mount, Jesus referred to a specific understanding of religion that needed deconstruction. The section begins with Jesus saying, "unless your righteousness far surpasses that of the scribes and Pharisees, you will not enter the kingdom of heaven" (Matthew 5:20). The scribes and Pharisees were the cream of the crop when it came to righteous living. Jesus said they needed to repent of that kind of thinking. Then he got specific.

You've been told that if you murder someone, you will have to answer to the court or stand trial. Jesus said murder is not the issue. The issue is anger. The Pharisees wanted to focus on doing (murder), and Jesus wanted to focus on being (angry).

Next, Jesus said to rethink adultery (Matthew 5:27). The problem is not the action but the thought of lust exposing adultery that has already occurred in the heart. It's better to pluck out an eye. Then Jesus turns to making false vows, and it's better not to swear by anything. He also speaks of revenge (Matthew 5:38) and hating enemies (Matthew 5:43). He turned all of these upsidedown and taught his disciples to deconstruct the faith they had been taught.

"You have heard..." but that's not correct. That is what is happening with deconstruction today. People are questioning if what they have always heard is correct. With over 2,000 years of history, the truth of what Jesus said has been covered by countless traditions and misconceptions. Many of the doctrines and practices that most of us were taught developed years after Jesus, many of them in response to world events.

We were taught that faithful Christians drive to a building on Sunday mornings and gather, sing songs, give an offering, and listen to a sermon. Have you ever given serious consideration to how or why those traditions developed? Think about it. Or, as Jesus would say, "repent" (change your mind) about what it means to be a faithful Christian. They may or may not be valid expressions of faith. Deconstruction means that we don't simply accept something as true because it's what everyone does.

Jesus used other metaphors of deconstruction, i.e., losing life to gain life, grain of wheat dying before growing. He was not afraid of giving serious thought to why we believe certain things. He did not hesitate to change the way scripture had always been interpreted and speak of the emptiness of religious practices and the weaknesses of religious leaders. I feel confident saying that Jesus intended to be more than an asterisk to Judaism. He called us to repent.

Even casual observers realize that Christianity needs deconstruction. The message of love and forgiveness that Jesus proclaimed has become anger and judgment. Jesus's hope for unity in His prayer for the church has devolved into thousands of denominations and sects. The concept of dying to self has been swallowed up by massive egos filling pulpits. The assignment to take the hope of the Gospel to the whole world has been a miserable failure.

Deconstruction seeks to understand what went wrong. The Christian religion is a fixer-upper in need of help.

Jesus and the Cross

We can't discuss Jesus without considering the cross. What was that about? Numerous Christians gather every Sunday and recite the Apostle's Creed

I believe in Jesus Christ, his only Son, our Lord,
who was conceived by the Holy Spirit
and born of the virgin Mary.
He suffered under Pontius Pilate,
was crucified, died, and was buried;
he descended to hell.
The third day he rose again from the dead.
He ascended to heaven
and is seated at the right hand of God the Father almighty.
From there he will come to judge the living and the dead.

We proclaim these words, but they don't explain how Jesus' death achieved our salvation. That is what the doctrine of atonement is all about. A simple definition is "at-one-ment." Atonement describes the meaning of Jesus' cross and what role it played in contributing to our fellowship with God. It is an attempt to explain the following:

Why did Jesus die on the cross?

How does His death make it possible for our sins to be forgiven?

If God is omnipotent, why couldn't He forgive our sins without Jesus' death?

Jesus provided numerous corrections of false beliefs:
- God needs a sacrifice for sin.
- God favors Israel over every other nation.
- God hates people who don't serve Him.
- God favors religious people.
- God favors wealthy people.
- God has cursed poor people.

Jesus also clarified other beliefs about sin:
- God considers lust equivalent to adultery.
- God considers hate equivalent to murder
- God wants us to turn the other cheek instead of fighting back.
- God wants us to give up our comfort to benefit others.
- God wants us to love our enemies.
- God wants us to forgive those who have wronged us.
- God wants us to trust Him for all our needs rather than worry.
- God wants us to treat others as we want to be treated.

All these understandings are found in Jesus' short Sermon on the Mount. He provided much more information, in fact, so much more, that "if they were written in detail, I expect that even the world itself would not contain the books that could be written" (John 21:25).

Instead of a vengeful, angry God seeking out people to punish for not living up to His standards, Jesus showed us that God is a father, waiting eagerly for a wandering child to return home. Once we come to our senses and realize that life is better in the father's house, we will go to Him. We don't go out of fear of punishment but in recognition of how much He loves us.

Once we accept the idea that God is not mad, we need to rethink what the cross was all about. If there was no need to pay a price for man's sins, then we need to *repent* (re-think) what we believe about Jesus' death. This process begins with listening to what Jesus said Himself. What happens on the cross is God's sovereign love; God commends His love toward us... It is God Himself on the cross.

Jesus declared that "the Son of Man has come to seek and to save that which was lost" (Luke 16:10). The word *save* carries the idea of bringing safety to someone and providing the means to cure, heal, or restore health. If we are saved, it means we have been restored, in this case, our relationship with God. Jesus came to restore the *lost* to God. Jesus constantly demonstrated this characteristic of God as He frequently healed the sick and drew close to sinners.

In the 15th chapter of Luke, Jesus told three parables about being lost—the lost sheep, the lost coin, and the lost (prodigal) son. The shepherd left the flock to find the stray sheep, and the woman swept the entire house to find the coin. The story of the Prodigal Son is the complete Gospel. As we noted earlier, the father was waiting expectantly for the son to return home, not with an offering or sacrifice, but with nothing more than a desire to be in the father's house.

In John 14:6, Jesus said, "I am the way, and the truth, and the life; no one comes to the Father except through Me." To return to the father, Jesus is necessary. Otherwise, we don't know how to get there. We will attempt to get to God laden with offerings and gifts. Jesus' way is that God is waiting for us to come home. The way to God is empty-handed. The prodigal in Jesus' parable did not need to bring a sacrifice; he just needed to go home. Jesus came to tell us that.

So, we still have the question of why did Jesus die? Why the cross?

The word *atone* means to make amends or reparation. The idea of finding a way to be right with God is the foundation behind all religions. Without atonement, humans would be eternally separate from God, and it's necessary because of sin. Remember, we learned with Adam's "sin" that it means to hide or turn away from God. Jesus showed up in a culture that was steeped in the notion that sin was atoned for by offering a blood sacrifice. Jewish life centered around the Temple in Jerusalem, where the offerings were made.

One theory, probably the one you grew up believing, is known as the Penal Substitutionary Theory of Atonement. The terms mean a penalty was to be paid, and a substitute made the payment. Because of sin, man was in debt and had to pay the penalty. One thread of the theory claims the debt was owed to Satan, like when you borrow money from a mobster; you owe a debt to the bad guy that has to be paid. The other thread in this theory is that the debt is owed to God; He is the one who is offended by our sin.

Jesus died to pay the penalty that we deserved. God provided the substitute by sending His son. Most of us have understood Jesus' death in this way since we were first introduced to the faith. Even the hymns we sang reinforced the idea, songs about the blood of Jesus and the cross. Even many contemporary songs pick up this idea of Jesus paying the debt for our sins. One popular contemporary song has the line, "I owed a debt I could not pay; He paid a debt He did not owe." Another claims, "Till on that cross as Jesus died, the wrath of God was satisfied."

The penal substitutionary theory reduces Jesus' life to one transaction that required three hours. Nothing else about His life matters and is diminished to nothing more than a preamble to create a situation where He would be put to death. It's a transaction because God is offering us a bargain—I'll pay for everything and give you eternal life, and all you need to do is believe in Jesus. That is how the church has presented the Gospel.

This understanding is built on the faulty belief that God is angry and demands payment for our sin. The theory solves the problem of guilt over sin, but it does nothing to restore our relationship. How many people do you know who declare their belief in Jesus but have zero relationship with God? It's like getting a great bargain on a new car but not driving it off the dealer's lot.

We have turned salvation into a magic trick. If we say, "hocus pocus," or in this case, the sinner's prayer, magic happens, and suddenly everything is right with God. As long as we hold on to the notion that God is angry and demands a penalty for sin, this is the best we can do.

However, the cross of Jesus was not transactional; it was transformative. We need to focus more on restoring our relationship with God. Restoration between God and humans was the purpose of Jesus showing up in Palestine. He came to "seek and to save" the lost (Jesus' words). His healing ministry provided a demonstration of that restoration. He never punished people; He challenged people to *repent*, re-think what they believed. He came to heal, not punish, because that's who God is. Richard Rohr points out that the cross is "a dramatic demonstration of God's outpouring love, meant to utterly shock the heart and turn it back toward trust and love of the Creator."

My father was a large man. He fought with the Marines in World War II and was wounded in the battle of Iwo Jima. He was the strongest man I ever knew, and I had a healthy fear, whether he was around or not. There was nothing more frightening than to hear my mother say, "We'll talk to your father when he gets home," or hear Him tell me after I had been disruptive in church, "We'll talk when we get home."

About the time I turned 17, I got a Driver's License. It was a great day that I wasn't sure would ever happen. Because of my polio, my legs were essentially useless, so it didn't seem I would be able to drive. One day my father came home and announced he had discovered a place that would install hand controls on the car that would allow me to drive. They are commonplace today, but in the late 1960s, not so much.

The car was outfitted, and I took Driver's Education at school, which was no small feat. The instructor had to drive me to our house so I could use our car. The car didn't have a brake on the instructor's side, so he had no way to stop me when I went wrong. Mr. Weigand went the extra mile to help me get a license.

Finally, it was official, and I could drive. One Wednesday night after church, my father handed the keys to me and told me I could drive home by myself. It was a short drive down Eppinger Blvd., and a right turn onto Russell Way, not more than a mile. My friend Jim Grundy lived along the way, so we agreed I could take him home.

When we got to the stop sign, Jim and I decided there was a girl we knew who really needed to see us; that's the way teenage boys think. Instead of turning right, we turned left and found ourselves on

Washington St., headed south. Waiting at a stoplight at 88th street, having a great time, Jim looked out his passenger's side window, turned to me, and said, "O no."

I looked over and saw my father. He was taking some kids home after church and happened to be going in the same direction. Jim rolled down the window. My father looked at me and said, "We'll talk when you get home."

I was afraid.

Remember, my father was a large man. He was an imposing figure, not just to me, but his strong personality made people notice when he was around. I had every reason to be afraid. But I wasn't afraid he would hurt me; that was the least of my fears. Allow me to explain why.

On a Sunday afternoon in 1968, I graduated from High School. That evening, I checked into the hospital for three surgeries scheduled for the next few weeks. The surgeries were designed to correct deformities in my back and both feet due to a serious bout of polio. They operated on my left foot on Monday, followed by the same procedure on my right foot on Wednesday. I had a cast up to my knee on both legs. On Friday, they strapped my head into a harness and hung me from the ceiling to straighten my back. Then they wrapped my entire body in plaster to keep my spine as straight as possible. A hinge was installed on the right side, and every day, Dr. Matchett turned the hinge to bend my spine a little more. The plan was to go until I said, "Enough, I can't take any more." At that point, bone was to be chipped out of my thigh and placed on my spinal cord to fuse it straight.

One afternoon after several weeks of twisting and hospital bed boredom, Dr. Matchett came into the room as my father was visiting. The doctor said he was concerned that I was so small and weak that he didn't think he could get enough bone from my thigh to do the fusion.

It's an understatement to say I was disappointed. A wasted summer stuck in a plaster cast.

Before I could give it much thought, my father spoke up and asked Dr. Matchett, "Can you take the bone from my leg?"

I need to tell you one more thing about my father. I mentioned he was wounded in the war. He lost his right leg. When he offered to give up bone from his leg, understand that he only had one leg.

The doctor thought for a moment and indicated he didn't see any reason why it wouldn't work (remember, this was the 1960s). They chiseled bone fragments from Daddy's leg and stuck them in my back, where they remain to this day. The surgery was much more painful and harder on him than me, but he never complained. In fact, for the rest of his life, he proudly told people that I was literally "bone of his bone."

That's the kind of father I had.

When I say I was afraid when he caught me driving in the wrong place, I wasn't afraid he would hurt or punish me. I was afraid I had disappointed him. That was the last thing I wanted to do, and when I let my teenage hormones and stupidity take over, that's what I did. I don't recall if we ever talked about anything when I got home. There was no need for him to say anything. I learned my lesson, and it has stayed with me since.

Proverbs 1:7 says, "The fear of the Lord is the beginning of knowledge." It doesn't mean that we are afraid of God. God told Abraham twice not to fear (Genesis 15:1; 26.24). Moses reminded the people not to be afraid (Exodus 14:13).

King Saul testified that he sinned because he "feared the people" instead of listening to God (1 Samuel 15:24). The Old Testament repeatedly identifies those who sin and do evil things as those who do not fear the Lord. It does not mean fear in the sense of punishment but of reverence and awe. They don't obey God because they do not venerate Him. Listen to the final words of the Old Testament: "Then those who feared the Lord spoke to one another, and the Lord listened attentively and heard *it*, and a book of remembrance was written before Him for those who fear the Lord and esteem His name. And they will be Mine, says the Lord of armies, on the day that I prepare *My* own possession, and I will have compassion for them just as a man has compassion for his own son who serves him. So you will again distinguish between the righteous and the wicked, between one who serves God and one who does not serve Him" (Malachi 3:16-18).

A significant flaw with Christianity is the notion that God is to be feared. Christ showed up in the form of a man named Jesus. He was God in the flesh, as John repeatedly called Him, the Word of God. Jesus was God speaking to us. Having a visible, audible expression of God is the key to understanding God and ought to be the key to interpreting scripture (i.e., what we call the Old Testament).

It was necessary for Jesus to walk the dusty Palestinian streets because man's ideas about God had become warped. According to the Genesis writer, it began early with Adam and Eve in the garden. When they disobeyed God, they hid in the bushes. After God put them in an ideal place, freely gave everything necessary, and even walked with them in the evenings, they misunderstood Him. They were afraid of God, but not like I was afraid of my father. I didn't run and hide. I didn't try to avoid him. I knew his heart, and being with him and doing his will was best for me. Any doubts I ever had about my father's love disappeared that day in the hospital when he willingly sacrificed himself for me. Jesus came to remove any doubts we have about God's love. "For God so loved the world, that He gave His only Son..." (John 3:16).

On the cross, Jesus was transforming our opinion about God. When Jesus was asked by the ruler how to be saved (Mark 10), He didn't say anything about believing anything. He was not asked to offer a prayer. Salvation is not a single act of confession but comes by following Jesus, and when we know God, we will follow Him, and He will lead us to God. Like the prodigal who "came to his senses" (Luke 15:17) and returned home to his father, on the cross, Jesus called us to return to our senses and return to the Father. Because I knew my earthly father and how much he loved me, I had little desire to wander away from him.

Some will be tempted to drag Paul's writings into this conversation. The problem is that Paul does not have a single theory of atonement. He uses at least six metaphors to describe the accomplishment of the cross of Jesus. Paul uses the term "sacrifice" (see 1 Corinthians 5:7) without connecting it to appeasing an angry God. Jesus was a sacrifice offered by God. When He sent His son with the task of communicating His desires, He knew humans would not receive Him well, even to the point of killing Him. Yet, He did it anyway. Jesus' death on the cross was God sacrificing Himself to help us understand His love for us.

Another metaphor used by Paul is that of a redeemer (see Galatians 3:13). Family members were often redeemed from slavery by a "redeemer" who paid the price. Think of it as what we might call slave trading. A slave is purchased, the price paid, but then the slave is set free. Christ was the redeemer, the cross was the price, and we, the freed slave.

Paul also used the idea of "justification" frequently in his writing (see Romans 5:9). It is the idea of being made right with God. The pneumonic device for justification is "just as if we never sinned." "Reconciliation" is another metaphor (see Ephesians 2:15-17). It means to be brought back into a relationship with God. The prodigal comes home; Adam is put back in the garden. The final metaphor is "adoption" (see Galatians 4:4-6). Through the cross, we are brought into a family where God is the loving parent.

It's important to remember Paul's cultural background. He was a Jew, steeped in the Jewish religion, even identifying himself as "a Hebrew of Hebrews; as to the Law, a Pharisee" (Philippians 3:5). It was natural for him to think in terms of Jesus as the fulfillment of Jewish law, meeting all the requirements expected from the promised Messiah. Instead of developing a complete understanding of the cross, he brings together all the consequences of what Jesus accomplished. Jesus sacrificed Himself; he is our redeemer, setting us free; we are now justified, reconciled, and adopted into God's family. Paul doesn't tell us how all this happened. That has been left to the theologians who have devised a plethora of theories. Any theory based on an angry God is flawed. That became clear when Jesus showed up to prove how much God loves us.

We can't leave Paul until we examine what he said in Romans 5:8-9:

"But God demonstrates His own love toward us, in that while we were yet sinners, Christ died for us. Much more then, having now been justified by His blood, we shall be saved from the wrath of God through Him."

In this passage, it says specifically that through the blood of Jesus, we will be saved from "the wrath of God." It seems we're back at square one and forget all the stuff I said about God not being angry.

However, that's not what Paul said. Paul didn't say Jesus saves us from the wrath of God. The two words "of God" were not written by Paul. You will notice that your translation has them in italics, meaning they were not in Paul's writing but added later for *clarity*. The words certainly clarify what someone meant, but it was someone other than Paul. Paul said Jesus saves us from "the wrath." If you continue reading, it's obvious that Paul meant death (see Romans 5:12-21). Jesus saved us from death, not God's wrath.

In the next chapter, Paul writes verse we are familiar with (Romans 6:23) and tells us the wages of sin is death. Jesus saved us from death which was the consequence of turning our back on God. God doesn't kill us because He's angry with us; we die because we chose to live outside of God's presence.

Now, back to the reason Jesus died on the cross. If God didn't kill Him, who did? The Gospel accounts are clear. The Romans, in cahoots with Jewish leaders, nailed Jesus on the cross. Humans killed him. Now the question is, why? If Jesus was such a great guy, why did they kill Him?

Jesus told His disciples that men would kill him (see Mark 9:31). The opposition to Jesus occurred early. "...the Jews were seeking all the more to kill Him, because He not only was breaking the Sabbath but also was calling God His own Father, making Himself equal with God. (John 5:18). This danger even impacted Jesus' ministry: "He was unwilling to walk in Judea because the Jews were seeking to kill Him" (John 7:1). After word spread that Jesus had raised Lazarus from the grave, things got serious.

Therefore the chief priests and the Pharisees convened a council and were saying, "What are we doing? For this man is performing many signs. If we let Him go on like this, all men will believe in Him, and the Romans will come and take away both our place and our nation." But one of them, Caiaphas, who was high priest that year, said to them, "You know nothing at all, nor do you take into account that it is expedient for you that one man die for the people, and that the whole nation not perish." Now he did not say this on his own initiative, but being high priest that year, he prophesied that Jesus was going to die for the nation, and not for the nation only, but in order that He might also gather together into one the children of God who are scattered abroad. So from that day on they planned together to kill Him. (John 11:47-53)

The reason they sought to kill Jesus was because He was a threat to their comfort and security. If enough people responded to Jesus' message, the Romans might retaliate, and they would lose their position as religious leaders. Jesus' message of God's love was a threat. Their religion was built on the concept that God was angry, hated sinners, and needed to be appeased. Israel developed an elaborate sacrificial system and religious structure based on this premise, so to be told that God loves sinners threw their entire world into question.

By the way, things are no different today. Many who read the pages of this book will be upset because I have questioned their sacred beliefs, beliefs they have held for as long as they can remember. Fortunately, I don't have the ability to influence many people, so the worst I will get is a few negative comments. It's a shame that the message that God loves us and doesn't want to condemn people to hell is so disturbing that people killed Him.

Several times, we referenced Jesus' parable of the prodigal son as the Gospel in story form. Jesus told another parable to explain why He was killed.

"Listen to another parable. There was a landowner who planted a vineyard and put a wall around it and dug a wine press in it, and built a tower, and rented it out to vine-growers and went on a journey. When the harvest time approached, he sent his slaves to the vine-growers to receive his produce. The vine-growers took his slaves and beat one, and killed another, and stoned a third. Again he sent another group of slaves larger than the first; and they did the same thing to them. But afterward he sent his son to them, saying, 'They will respect my son.' But when the vine-growers saw the son, they said among themselves, 'This is the heir; come, let us kill him and seize his inheritance.' They took him, and threw him out of the vineyard and killed

A Better Understanding of Love and Frogiveness

him. Therefore when the owner of the vineyard comes, what will he do to those vine-growers?" They said to Him, "He will bring those wretches to a wretched end, and will rent out the vineyard to other vine-growers who will pay him the proceeds at the proper seasons."

Jesus said to them, "Did you never read in the Scriptures, 'The stone which the builders rejected, This became the chief corner stone; This came about from the Lord, And it is marvelous in our eyes?

Therefore I say to you, the kingdom of God will be taken away from you and given to a people, producing the fruit of it. And he who falls on this stone will be broken to pieces; but on whomever it falls, it will scatter him like dust."

When the chief priests and the Pharisees heard His parables, they understood that He was speaking about them. When they sought to seize Him, they feared the people, because they considered Him to be a prophet. (Matthew 21:33-46).

Jesus died on the cross because He was a threat to turn things upside down. If you don't think that's reason enough, try to change the status quo of something. It can be your church, your family, your work environment, or your civic organization. It doesn't matter, people don't want to change, and the ones most resistant to change are those who are in control of the current situation. When Jesus came with a new message about God, He upset the whole world, especially those in charge, and it got Him killed.

After all that, here's the gospel message in a thumbnail. Jesus shows us that God loves us and wants to have a relationship with us. The way that happens is to listen to Jesus' words and follow His example. Or, as Jesus said Himself, *"For God so loved the world, that He gave His only begotten Son, that whoever believes in Him shall not perish, but have eternal life. For God did not send the Son into the world to judge the world, but that the world might be saved through Him. He who believes in Him is not judged; he who does not believe has been judged already because he has not believed in the name of the only begotten Son of God. This is the judgment that the Light has come into the world, and men loved the darkness rather than the Light, for their deeds were evil. For everyone who does evil hates the Light and does not come to the Light for fear that his* deeds will be exposed. But he who practices the truth comes to the Light, so that his deeds may be manifested as having been wrought in God." (John 3:16-21)

Jesus' words are so clear it's hard to understand how it can be missed. The key is believing Jesus. Believing His message that God is not angry but loves us. Believing His message that God wants us to live in the light. Believing His message that He wants us to "practice the truth."

The Resurrection

The story of Jesus doesn't end on the cross. Paul understood this clearly when he wrote, "if Christ has not been raised, then our preaching is vain, your faith also is vain" (1 Corinthians 15:14). Later in the paragraph, he adds, "if Christ has not been raised, your faith is worthless; you are still in your sins" (v.17). Remember, Jesus came to defeat death, in other words, to give us eternal life. If His life ended on the cross, then He obviously lacked the power of eternal life.

My point in this short section is not to provide empirical proof that Jesus came back to life after being dead for three days. I'm beginning with the belief that He did, just as reported in the Gospels. The fact that people claim it's a physical impossibility makes no difference; we're talking about God, after all.

It was not Jesus on the cross that defeated death; it was the resurrection. He overcame death. Because He defeated death, we do not need to fear death. We know Jesus can keep His promise of eternal life because He has done it before. I have written more than 25 books and helped more than 100 other writers publish their books. If you want to know how to write or publish a book, ask me. I know how to do that.

In the same way (only greater), if you want to know how to defeat death, look to Jesus. He has been there and done that. That's why Easter has always been the pinnacle of the Christian calendar. Interestingly, the cross has become the primary symbol of Christianity, perhaps because it's not easy to symbolize an empty tomb. However, the cross would be meaningless and powerless without the empty tomb.

In that same 15ᵗʰ chapter of 1 Corinthians, Paul speaks of how death is swallowed up in the victory of Christ's resurrection and lost its sting. Then listen to this, "The power of death is sin (missing the mark), and the ruler of sin is the law" (my translation of 1 Corinthians 15:56). The scourge of death that has been with us since Adam is no longer a problem. Jesus has given us life.

Luke recorded the risen Christ's final words: "So it is written, that the Christ would suffer and rise from the dead on the third day, and that repentance for forgiveness of sins would be proclaimed in His name to all the nations, beginning from Jerusalem. You are witnesses of these things. And behold, I am sending the promise of My Father upon you; but you are to stay in the city until you are clothed with power from on high" (Luke 24:46-49).

Did you catch the last part where He instructed them to hang around for something more? That's where we are going next in our history of God.

Part 4: God's Desire
Eternal by Transformation

We $noted$ at the outset that God is spirit. Speaking to the Samaritan woman, Jesus said that "God is spirit" (John 4:24). A spirit is without substance or material matter. A spirit cannot be experienced by any of our five senses. Although we might speak of "hearing" the Spirit, we don't really mean an audible sound. The same is true if we speak of "feeling" the Spirit. We do not really feel a touch on our skin. These are inner experiences, not encountered by one of our five senses.

The Greek word translated as spirit means wind or breath. It's like trying to define a gentle spring breeze. You can't see, hear, smell, or taste it, but you know it's there (although I admit, you can slightly feel it). The spirit can't be quantified or measured.

When God (spirit) created man (physical), He breathed into him the breath of life, and man became a living person (Genesis 2:7). It is the spirit that gives us life. When the body dies, the spirit either dies with it or moves on to something else. That "something else" is the holy grail of religious questions.

I don't have any statistics, but I'm confident a significant majority of humans over the years have believed that life continues even after the body dies. Some have the belief that the spirit recycles and reincarnates into another form of existence until advancing into a higher state. Others have the belief that every person goes to either a good place or a bad place, heaven or hell. Of course, this is the common Christian doctrine. It essentially boils down to those who believe in Jesus will live eternally in heaven, and those who don't will spend eternity in hell.

I indicated earlier it was when I became uncomfortable with the notion of God sending the bulk of humanity into a fiery torture chamber for eternity that was like a booster rocket to deconstructing my faith. I couldn't find a way to reconcile the belief that God is love and that God sends most people to a place far worse than a Nazi prison camp. Logic dictates that if there is no hell, then there are only two options – heaven or ceasing to exist.

Jesus spoke a great deal about eternal life, but He told us very little about what that means. Countless books have been written on the subject, but honestly, God doesn't tell us much. Most of what we think about heaven is mere speculation, and it's not surprising that most of what we expect to find there is nothing more than our ideal version of what life on earth would be. I don't know, but I lean toward the idea it will be an entirely different kind of existence.

Since neither you nor I know much about the future, let's focus on the work of God's Spirit in the present. The idea of God breathing His Spirit into us suggests that He is alive in us. If we can understand the ramifications of God in us, it will revolutionize how we live. The most basic thing we know is that the Spirit is within us. "Do you not know that you are a temple of God and that the Spirit of God dwells in you?" (1 Corinthians 3:16)

Writer Jim Palmer paints the picture like this:

Jesus spoke to them, saying it was time for him to leave. His friends were distraught upon hearing this news. They said in disbelief, "You cannot go, Jesus. How shall we carry on without you?"

Jesus replied, "You must find me in yourself."

"How is that possible?" one said. "Will you step inside us, and live your life there?"

Jesus explained, "The life you have seen in, as, and through me is also your life. We share in that one life together. If I stay longer you will become convinced that this is about me, and miss the life I am referring to, which is also in, as, and through you."

After a few moments of silence, one of them asked Jesus, "But should we not elevate you to the highest place among men and worship you?"

"Only do as I did, and heed that life and spirit that is within you. Listen to its promptings. Follow what it shows and tells you. This is the way."

After speaking these words, Jesus turned and walked away. At some distance one of them called out, "But Jesus, should the world not know about you?" He stopped and turned, and said with compassion in his eyes, "Don't you see? This was never about me. It was always you. You be Jesus now."

After His resurrection and ascension, we were not left alone. The Holy Spirit, God's empowering presence, is with us giving us everything we need. As Palmer says, we are now able to be Jesus in the world. We are not Jesus, but God is within us. Listen to how Paul describes it: "...the mystery which had been hidden from the past ages and generations, but now has been revealed to His saints, to whom God willed to make known what the wealth of the glory of this mystery among the Gentiles is, the mystery that is Christ in you, the hope of glory. We proclaim Him, admonishing every person and teaching every person with all wisdom, so that we may present every person complete in Christ. For this purpose I also labor, striving according to His power which works mightily within me" (Colossians 1:26-29).

The mystery that has now been revealed is that Christ is in us. It is God's Spirit within us that makes us alive. When we are given new life, we are sent back into the world, but we are not sent empty-handed. We are now Christ in the world, and we have the opportunity to be Jesus to others.

Think about what that means. I had the following conversation on Facebook recently and it caused me to think. She was trying to complain about a meme I had posted and what she wanted from me had nothing to do with the original post.

Other Person: I'm curious. How do you define "christianity?"
Me: The same way Jesus and Paul defined it.
Other Person: There is no record of either Paul or Jesus defining or even using the word. You opened this can of worms, Terry. Deconstruct, dude! Define "christianity."

Me: *That was my point. Neither Jesus nor Paul used the term so why do you? By the way, "dude" doesn't sound very respectful. Not a term used by Jesus or Paul either.*

Other Person: *I used the word, dude, because you are just being evasive...*

Me: *Like Jesus and Paul, I did not use the word "Christianity." You brought it into the conversation, you define it. So, the word "dude" means "evasive"???*

Ok, so maybe I was being a little cantankerous. But I was trying to get her to think rather than spout off words without thought. I will also admit she caused me to do some thinking as well with her question, "How do you define christianity," although she spelled it in a lower case.

It is true that neither Jesus nor Paul ever used the term *Christian* or *Christianity*. The word does appear three times in the Bible, twice in Acts and once in 1 Peter. Barnabas and Paul worked in Antioch for a year, teaching people about Christ, and it was there the disciples were first called *Christians*. The second time was at Paul's trial before the Roman, Agrippa. Paul obviously presented a good case for the faith because Agrippa declared, "In a short time you are going to persuade me to make a Christian of myself" (Acts 26:28).

The third usage of the term is 1 Peter 4:16. The context is potential suffering and persecution, and believers must be careful that it's not because it is deserved due to immoral living. However, if "anyone suffers as a Christian, he is not to be ashamed." The word used in each instance is the same and means *like Christ*. Those who became known as followers of Christ were labeled as Christians, and then Peter adopted the term to refer to fellow believers.

Other terms used in the New Testament were disciples, believers, the Lord's disciples, and those who belonged to the Way. Peter seems to be the first (at least in writing) to apply the term *Christian* to himself and others. Remember, this is the same man who denied Christ three times on the night of the crucifixion. He grew to the point of being able to say if we do suffer for being a Christian, don't be ashamed but "glorify God in this name" (1 Peter 4:16). In other words, he glorified God that he was labeled a Christian.

How to Become a Christian

Many Christians today define a Christian as someone who has been saved. As we have noted, Paul used the phrase *in Christ* instead. This is why I can say that we can *be Jesus* in the world because that is essentially who we are. People who encountered the earthly Jesus were not sequestered in a holy place. They were always sent off with the power of their new relationship with God back into their world. We are not saved to sit and enjoy Jesus; we are sent to be Jesus.

The answer to the great question of how to be saved was supposed to be easy. They said to "invite Jesus into your heart when I was a kid." It sounded good, but I wasn't sure what that meant. To be honest, I still have no clue what that means—inviting Jesus into your heart?

As I got older, the answer changed to confess your sin, ask for forgiveness, and pledge your faith in Jesus. That was a simple enough process—Romans 3:23, then Romans 6:23, then Romans 5:8, and finally Romans 10:13. Tack on a quick prayer, and you're saved.

When I became a pastor, I was guilted into accepting the responsibility to teach everyone how to get others to say the *Sinner's Prayer.* You know the one where you say something like, *"Lord, I admit I am a sinner. I accept Your death as the penalty for my sin and recognize that Your mercy and grace are a gift You offer to me because of Your great love, not based on anything I have done. Cleanse me and make me Your child. By faith, I receive You into my heart as the Son of God and as Savior and Lord of my life. In Your precious name, Amen."*

It soon became apparent this was a big task. First, I had to convince people, many of them too shy to speak to a stranger, that God wanted them to approach people with a clear presentation of the Gospel. Needless to say, that didn't happen. I wasn't any more comfortable, but I occasionally mustered the courage to give it a shot.

Once I found a weak-minded believer willing to learn the process, it was necessary to spend several hours teaching them how to do better than Paul's 81 words from the Roman Road. It usually required memorizing multiple pages of script and scripture. It often felt like it would be easier to find the Holy Grail than to explain how to be saved.

After some time, it got frustrating. There has to be a better way. Finally, I did what I should have done from the outset—I decided to see how Jesus would answer the question of how to be saved if he was ever asked. Sure enough, there it was. You know the story. A young man came to Jesus and asked what he needed to do to obtain eternal life (Matthew 19:16). That's close enough.

This man was accustomed to getting what he wanted; the rich usually do. Also, he had already tried the religious route, professing that he had kept the rules his entire life. This would be akin to a wealthy deacon coming into the preacher's office with a question about salvation. The preacher reaches into his seminary bag of tricks. Out comes the plan of salvation. The problem is that the deacon has already been down that religious road, and it wasn't enough. Jesus knew that. He corrected the man's thinking, casting aside all the religious stuff, and told him salvation is simple. He had to get rid of all his stuff because it was what the man served; many rich men do. Once that was out of the way, all he had to do was follow Jesus.

If Jesus said following Him was all that was necessary to be saved, it should be good enough for me as well. With that in mind, here is the simple Gospel: Follow Jesus!

God, the creator of man, has always sought to have a relationship with man. The Bible says that He spent time with the first humans, Adam and Eve, in the garden. However, after they violated God's one prohibition, they hid from God and ended up being excluded from the garden. Their sin broke their relationship with God.

God's love for man never changed. Like a parent with a wayward child, God anxiously waited for man to return home. It didn't happen for thousands of years (time is not that meaningful to God), so God had to do something to bring man back home for fellowship.

It was clear that man did not come home because he didn't fully understand God's love. The Old Testament says little about God's love, forgiveness, or grace. Therefore, God did the most loving thing possible; He sent His Son (Himself in a human body) to tell man what He was really like.

Jesus told a parable about a landowner who planted a vineyard and leased it to vine-growers (Matthew 21). At harvest time, he sent servants to collect his portion, but the tenants beat and killed the servants. Two times he sent servants, and two times they were rebuffed. Finally, he chose to send his son, thinking they would respect him. Instead, realizing the son was the heir, they killed him to take the inheritance for themselves. The religious leaders did to God's Son the same thing the tenants in Jesus' story did to the vineyard owner's son.

Jesus knew He was going to die at the hands of men. He gave Himself willingly because the message of God's love compelled Him to give everything so men would understand. The cross was not an altar used by God to pay for sin. God didn't need restitution for sin. All He wanted was for man to come home. In another of His stories, Jesus told of the prodigal son who left his father's home thinking he would be better off. He wasn't. After "he came to his senses" (Luke 12:17), he realized his father's house was the best place for him. His plan was to throw himself at his father's feet, confess his sin, and beg for forgiveness.

However, before he could say anything, the father saw him coming, ran down the road to greet him, and embraced and kissed him. The son quickly asked for forgiveness, but the way the story is told, the father wasn't even listening; he was planning a party. "...this son of mine was dead and has come to life again, he was lost and has been found" (Luke 12:24). Then they partied.

That is the Gospel. God loves you and is waiting for you to come home. Don't bring an offering, don't get your life straight, don't mend fences; just go to the father. Jesus said, "everyone who believes will have eternal life" (John 3:15). That's why Jesus frequently called people to follow Him. He wanted them to see God, to know God's love. When we know Jesus, we know God.

The Gospel is simple. Jesus will lead you to where life is best for you. Follow Him, and you will be saved. Jesus repeated the call, "follow me," over and over, but we missed it:

- To Peter and Andrew (Matthew 4:19)
- The potential disciple (Matthew 8:22)
- Matthew (Matthew 9:9)
- Anyone who doesn't follow is "not worthy" (Matthew 10:38)
- To anyone willing (Matthew 16:24)
- Questioning rich man (Matthew 19:21)
- Assurance that Peter did follow (Matthew 19:28)
- John the Baptizer's disciples (John 1:37)
- Phillip (John 1:43)
- Puts in the light (John 8:12)
- "My sheep...follow me (John 10:27)
- "If anyone serves Me, he must follow Me" (John 12:26)
- "If anyone loves Me, he will follow My word" (John 14:23)
- "The one who does not love Me does not follow My words (John 14:24)
- To Peter at the Last Supper (John 21:19)
- To Peter, who was worried about others (John 21:23)

In addition to Jesus calling people to follow Him, people did. Not only did the Twelve follow him, but continually large crowds followed him.

So, let's do it like Jesus. If you want to be saved, follow Jesus. Although Jesus proclaimed people forgiven, I can't find a recorded instance where anyone sought forgiveness from Jesus. Yet, most of our evangelism strategies begin by dealing with sin—admit you're a sinner and then ask for forgiveness. Another feature of our Gospel strategies requires praying to be saved. Again, Jesus never led anyone in prayer to be saved.

We prefer to boil the Gospel down to a simple formula that can be memorized, repeated, and easily shared. It makes life easier. Following Jesus can be messy; Jesus Himself was messy much of the time. He enjoyed *sinners*, broke rules, spoke out against religious leaders, and wasn't much of a *church-goer*. Following Him can be an adventure, and most of us prefer something more comfortable.

If you tell people they can be saved by reciting a prayer or by following Jesus, don't be surprised if they opt for the simple prayer. The result is that we have many people who think they have reservations in heaven but little interest in following Jesus. We have failed to understand that Jesus is attractive, and if we make Him known, crowds will follow.

How to Be a Christian

Paul offered a great prayer for believers for that purpose: "That is why I kneel before Abba God, from whom every family in heaven and on earth takes its name. And I pray that God, out of the riches of divine glory, will strengthen you inwardly with power through the working of the Spirit. May Christ dwell in your hearts through faith, so that you, being rooted and grounded in love, will be able to grasp fully the breadth, length, height and depth of Christ's love and, with all God's holy ones, experience this love that surpasses all understanding, so that you may be filled with all the fullness of God. To God—whose power now at work in us can do immeasurably more than we ask or imagine—to God be glory in the Church and *in Christ* Jesus through all generations, world without end! Amen" (Ephesians 3:14-21).

He is praying that we will live out the spiritual life given to us by God's infilling Spirit. This is important because many are hesitant to accept the idea that following Jesus is enough. They are concerned that if God doesn't spell out some rules to keep or changes to make, we won't know how to behave. Having a list of do's and don'ts is how we know what it means to follow Jesus. But the reason we don't need rules and regulations is because we have God's Spirit.

In the most frequently quoted verse of the Bible, John 3:16, Jesus promised eternal life to those who believe in Him. This is accomplished by instilling within us something that is eternal—the Spirit of God. Our lives are transformed, not because we suddenly decide to keep God's law or commandments, but because we are transformed by God's Spirit. While He was still in human form, Jesus said, "I will ask the Father, and He will give you another Helper, so that He may be with you forever; the Helper is the Spirit of truth, whom the world cannot receive, because it does not see Him or know Him; but you know Him because He remains with you and will be in you... I will not leave you as orphans; I am coming to you. But the Helper, the Holy Spirit whom the Father will send in My name, He will teach you all things, and remind you of all that I said to you" (John 14:16-18, 26).

True to His word, before departing, He fulfilled the promise. "So Jesus said to them again, 'Peace be to you; just as the Father has sent Me, I also send you.' And when He had said this, He breathed on them and said to them, 'Receive the Holy Spirit'" (John 20:22). God's Spirit now lives within us. God has not changed. We have been changed.

At some point, all of creation will be redeemed, but we have a head start. "For we know that the whole creation groans and suffers the pains of childbirth together until now. And not only that, but also we ourselves, having the first fruits of the Spirit, even we ourselves groan within ourselves, waiting eagerly for our adoption as sons and daughters, the redemption of our body. For in hope we have been saved, but hope that is seen is not hope; for who hopes for what he already sees? (Romans 8:22-24). It is stated even more clearly in 1 Corinthians - "... your body is a temple of the Holy Spirit within you, whom you have from God" (6:19).

Our excursion into the Brief History of God began with a look back —who is God and where did humans come from. We discovered that God created us for the purpose of fellowship (communion) with Him. From the beginning, God made every effort to make that clear and to keep humans from walking away from Him. He even went so far as to send Himself (His Son) to explain and demonstrate how He loves us.

Now, God lives on. Within us.

Genesis begins with the creation of the world. Revelation ends with the creation of a new world (Revelation 21-22). Perhaps a better title for this book would be "A Brief History of God and Humans." God's history never ends. Since God's Spirit now lives within us, neither does ours.

Conclusion

Far back in the introduction, I mentioned writing a biography for Erik Daniels. You remember, the young man who lived a violent, drug-filled life. He killed three people. The first victim was Erik's grandfather. After two years of being sexually abused several times a week, Erik grabbed a kitchen knife and stabbed him more than 30 times. While in prison, he made a friend who was heavily involved in the drug world. Once released, Erik jumped into that world with both feet, having nowhere else to go.

Erik was caught by the DEA. He had no choice but to testify against his partners, but he refused to enter the Witness Protection Program, choosing instead to hide. The second person he killed was a young woman who discovered his identity. Although Erik had no reason to believe she would expose him, out of fear of the possibility, he killed her and hid her body in the deep forest of Oregon. The third victim foolishly confronted him at a drunken party.

Despite his violent life, Erik had a winsome personality. I liked him. We never met in person, and I know nothing about his appearance. Something he said in one of our initial conversations has stuck with me for several years.

"My grandmother always told me that she believed I was an angel from heaven. I never really believed it, but when you look back, I should be dead, more than dead. I should be in prison, but I'm not. I don't know if God really had something, and I was too stupid to ever follow it or what, but my Grandmother was convinced God had some huge plan I was supposed to fill, and then she died, and I messed it all up and who would ever use me for anything...."

These words are a direct quote from Erik. It's a vivid memory that Erik spoke about two times in our conversations. It's apparent to me that he had given his grandmother's opinion some thought and came to reject it as pure nonsense, but I haven't been able to let it go that easily.

When I think back to Erik's introduction of his grandmother into the story, it's obvious that she was not a gentle, matronly woman that the word *grandmother* often conjures in our minds. She was a hard-working, hard-driving woman who shocked him with an over-familiarity with death. She killed a cow he loved without warning right in front of him. She also remained silent for two years as his grandfather sexually assaulted him at night.

Obviously, I don't consider his grandmother as any kind of prophet or spokeswoman for God. She was not the kind of woman we should turn to for spiritual guidance. However, there was some reason Erik remembered the words quoted above. The idea that God had something special for Erik would not go away even after learning about the horribly unproductive life he lived.

I am well aware that God frequently uses broken people to accomplish great things. The first one who comes to mind is Samson. Samson had squandered the blessings God had given him out of lust for a woman. He gave everything away because he couldn't say no to temptation. Yet, even after his enemies captured him, blinded him, and chained him up for mockery and ridicule, God used him in a way that causes us to retell his story. There was nothing in Samson's life that would indicate he could be employed by God.

Numerous biblical characters were broken by life. What about Moses, who was set adrift in the river as an infant, or Isaac, lain out on an altar staring at his father's hand with a knife set to plunge into his heart, or David, who was such an inconsequential person to his father that he wasn't considered worthy of meeting God's prophet. Do you see what I mean? None of us make it through life unbroken.

The difference between most of us and Erik is that even though we were broken at some point, we had someone in our life who came along and mended us. Such was not the case with Erik. He went from one abusive situation to another. It would have been like my father taking his Oldsmobile to the junkyard instead of the mechanic, and while at the junkyard, people kept coming along and taking all the parts. Erik never left the junkyard. He was continually broken and had no opportunity for repair.

At this point, let me explain my personal opinion of Erik. I only knew him for barely more than a month and never met him face to face. We spent many hours talking on the phone, and I've listened to those conversations over and over. However, I'm confident that at the time of his death, his wife might have been the only person who knew him better. As we waded through his life story, he never once mentioned anyone who was ever a friend. He never spoke of a person who cared about him for anything other than what they could get from him. I suspect that's why he liked me as well as he did. I truly cared for him, and he knew that.

My first impression of Erik, before I heard his story, was that he put his life together and was a success at something. He had money; he was well-spoken. In fact, one day, I even asked him where he was educated. He had a good command of the English language, spoke without any type of regional brogue, and used little slang. He was educated in prison, is what he told me. He didn't have many classroom opportunities in his life, but he said the teachers he did have typically told him he was a good learner. He also indicated that he liked to read, which might be the best way for anyone to get a good education.

I do know that when he became interested in a subject, he was tenacious to learn as much as fast as possible. He peppered me with questions about book marketing and publishing. Within a week, he knew more than I do about publicists and agents. He spoke to several and piqued their interest in our project. He convinced a well-known publicist to read the first chapter of the book, something that many authors are unable to do after years of trying.

There was a simple kindness about Erik that you sometimes see in young children. During our first few conversations, he continually apologized for things. He would frequently say, "I'm sorry..." and then proceed to tell me something, even when he had done nothing wrong. After a while, I just flat-out told him to quit apologizing. "You need to stop saying I'm sorry all the time," I said. "When you've done something wrong, that's fine, but otherwise, I don't want to hear it." Of course, he apologized, but then he quit.

He was also willing to learn. I could tell he was serious most of the time; I told him that one of the three things about life that I know for sure is that people need to laugh more. He said that he would work on it. A few days later, he told me that he was playing on the floor with his children, and his wife Kylie said there was something different about him. She affirmed that normally when he played with the children, he would be distracted, not really enjoying the time. However, on this particular occasion, he was sincerely laughing and having fun. He then thanked me for telling him to laugh more.

Erik lived the last decade of his life in hiding from people who were anxious to kill him. He had learned how to change his identity and practice deception. There was never any reason for him to lie about anything to me. If he did make up the whole thing, he had a great imagination, and he's an idiot for making himself out to be such an evil man. I have no doubt the story is true, perhaps embellished a bit like all of us do when we tell stories of our past.

At one point, I asked Erik if he thought he would ever kill anyone again. Without hesitation, he replied that it was something in his past and that it would never happen again. He really felt like he had changed. If you look back over the three times he killed someone, it was either at a moment of survival or rage. None of them were premeditated. He was convinced he had moved past that flaw in his personality.

However, about a week later, he had an occasion to call his mother on the phone. He was trying to secure some old photos that he might want to put in the book, so even though he hadn't spoken to her in years, he thought he would ask. It turned out to be a long-convoluted process where he posed as a private investigator working for her son and an elaborate made-up story. In the end, while on the phone, he identified himself to his mother, and she cussed him out and called him all kinds of unimaginable names. When Erik told me about the incident, he said, "You remember when I told you I would never kill anyone again? I was wrong."

At that moment, he realized he still had a problem with rage. It was caused by the one person in his life who should have been loving and supportive—his mother. This was the final contact they ever had with one another, and it ended in bitterness and anger. He was still broken, and the one who first broke him was the culprit.

I don't believe in coincidences. I am convinced that God brings people into our lives for a reason, and I pray every day for an opportunity to make a difference in someone's life. Erik finding me was not an accident nor a coincidence. I struggle to figure out the purpose.

Somewhere buried deep in his memory bank was his grandmother's notion that God had a plan for his life. Then he came to me to write his story. I asked him why he chose me because I knew he had other options. He said he had looked at my website and read some of my stuff and liked what he discovered. You don't have to see very much of what I have written to realize most of it is from a Christian perspective. I have been quite open through my writing about my faith. I would think that my religious background and experience would turn away someone like Erik, but it didn't. There must be a reason that goes beyond him simply liking my style.

I'm positive of some things this experience was NOT about. It was not about Erik, or someone like him, *finding Jesus*. I'm not saying that would not be great. I won't even deny that I prayed that he would find the spiritual life that only Jesus provides. But I don't think that was the purpose of our encounter. Erik was not attracted to me because he was seeking salvation. He was not looking for a *holy man* to restore his soul. There was not one moment when I felt like he had an interest in spiritual matters.

As often as Erik had been locked up, I'm confident he had heard the Gospel several times. Christians are quite active in prison ministries, and many inmates are vocal in sharing their faith with other inmates. I am not saying I had no intention of sharing the Gospel with Erik at some point. I did. I knew the time wasn't right now, but it would be eventually, but it never arrived. Even through all my grief over Erik's death, I never felt guilt or remorse for not breaking out the *Four Spiritual Laws* or leading him down the *Roman Road*.

Nor do I think the purpose was for someone to have the opportunity to convince Erik he was a bad person. He already knew that. He knew more than anyone that much of the stuff he had done was wrong, and he mentioned several times that the people he harmed didn't deserve what happened to them. I'm confident Erik didn't tell me everything he had done because it defied explanation. There was one episode he described to me, but the next day he asked me not to use it. It was bad enough in his mind that he didn't want Kylie to know.

I believe the purpose of the relationship between Erik and me was not for any of the above reasons, but I don't mean to suggest that there was not a spiritual purpose. I gained a much better understanding of what it means to be broken. Erik was by far the most broken person I have ever known. He didn't need religion, rules, or rituals; he needed more, and I could offer more. He needed to know that God loved him, and the only way I could explain that to him was by loving him.

Whenever my broken parts reared their ugliness, many people helped me put things back together, and I experienced healing of my soul. Whenever I have been broken, someone has always been there to put me back together. The same is true for most of us to some extent. You might not have been quite as fortunate as me, but you probably had folks who cared for you and tried to steer you in the right direction, people who would put you back together and kept you from being tossed on the scrap heap. Without these people, we would be useless.

Erik didn't have anyone like this in his life. From birth, he was an inconvenience to his mother, forcing her to endure an extra month of pregnancy because he wouldn't come out. His stepfather hated him and began to beat him at an early age. Even his siblings took every opportunity to make life difficult for Erik.

As he grew up, he never found that person who would be able to help him. The closest thing he ever had was his friend Derrick who was merely grooming him to be a part of his drug business. In the end, Derrick and his skinhead brothers are the ones who would be more than happy to kill Erik.

Are some people broken beyond repair? I don't know. It's hard to imagine anyone being more broken than Erik, yet I think there was still the opportunity for repair for him. It might be that time ran out for him at age 39, but I think he was still seeking, and I know that I was willing to help in any way possible. He chose to spend the final part of his life telling his story. Was he still looking for someone to accept him?

During my short relationship with Erik, I learned a great deal about loving the unlovable. Some of the things he told me were hard to hear, but I made a deliberate decision at the beginning that I was not going to judge him or offer my assessment of his life. Instead, I chose to love him to the best of my ability. I was determined to be non-judgmental.

One of the most valuable lessons I have learned in my life is that it is not my job to judge another person or the way they live. That work belongs to God. If God wants to condemn someone, He doesn't need my help. All I have been asked to do is love them. Some people read the Bible and focus on Jesus' condemnation of sin and the harsh judgments of God described in the Old Testament. Jesus might have condemned sin, and God might have been harsh at times, but that responsibility was never passed on to me. My goal with Erik was to convince him that someone loved him, and eventually, that would open the door for him to see that God loves him as well. Unfortunately, death came before I got to see that happen.

A friend suggested that Erik's story was a confession. That might explain why he turned to me, a religious man, perhaps seeking absolution for his sins. That idea resonates with me on several levels. His story was an extended confession of sorts. There was never a hint of pride in what he had done or bragging about his accomplishments. On the other hand, there were few expressions of contrition or sorrow for what he had done.

I don't know if he was seeking forgiveness or absolution. If he was, I'm afraid he died too soon. By the way, he knew he was dying, but he thought he had more than six weeks. He told me that doctors said it would take six months, but he felt he wouldn't be around quite that long, perhaps four or five. If he could have lasted another month or two, he might have been able to realize absolution and forgiveness from God.

When Erik died, I could have simply walked away from the story and quit the writing process. It was, after all, his story, not mine. However, I couldn't do that because his story had actually become my story. The experiences he related were so out of the ordinary for me that I spent a lot of time reflecting on what this whole thing was about.

I invested heavily in trying to understand Erik, and I couldn't simply leave him once he took his final breath.

Erik had been given a death sentence—not by a judge but by a doctor. Once that happened, all he wanted to do was tell his story in his words. As he said at the outset, he wanted to write a *tell-all* book.

I plan to keep the recordings and play them occasionally, at least the first part of every conversation that always went the same. The phone rings, and Erik answers. I say, "Hi, Erik."

He replies, "Hey young man, how 'ya doing?"

He always sounded happy to hear my voice, and he always called me "young man" even though he knew I was old enough to be his father. My biggest regret in our entire relationship is that he died before I could introduce him to my heavenly Father, the One who had been waiting eagerly for the prodigal to return home.

Like you and me, Erik was created for a relationship with God. That's what we are told throughout the whole Bible. Because we had a hard time understanding God, He came to us personally, in the form of Jesus (Son), to make it as clear as possible. Then, He planted Himself (Spirit) within us so we would have a relationship with Him for eternity.

Erik is the epitome of the thesis of my entire book. There was something deep within the most broken individual I have ever known that suggested he knew something about God. It was nothing more than an off-hand remark by his grandmother, but it stuck to him just like God sticks with all of us. In his mind, God had a "huge plan for his life." He had no idea what it was or how to find it, but he never forgot about it.

I have referenced Jesus' parable of the Prodigal Son several times. It encapsulates the purpose of Jesus showing up on earth. Up until now, our focus has been on the younger son, the one who left the father. As you know, there are two sons in the story. The older brother stayed at home and played the role of the dutiful son. In Jesus' story, the son describes his role and relationship with the father. "Look! For so many years I have been serving you and I have never neglected a command of yours; and yet you never gave me a young goat, so that I might celebrate with my friends; but when this son of yours came, who has devoured your wealth with prostitutes, you slaughtered the fattened calf for him'" (Luke 12:29-30).

If your understanding of God doesn't have an explanation that makes sense of Erik's life, then you need a bigger God. God loved Erik as much as He love me. God forgave Erik, just like He forgive me. When I wrote Erik's story, I gave it the title, "Broken, The Life and Times of Erik Daniels." He was broken, but all of us are broken to some extent. They only thing that kept him from being fixed is that nobody ever showed him what it felt like to be loved by God. That's what Jesus was all about.

The role of the older brothers is important to my story. Those who will have difficulty with what I have written are not people who don't know anything about God or people, like my short-term friend Erik. The ones I will hear from and be criticized by are the older brothers. The ones who have been living in the Father's house all along.

Jesus began His ministry with a call to *repent*. Remember, the word means to change your mind, to change the way you've been thinking. The history of God has been terribly misunderstood over the centuries by many. They didn't rethink their understanding of God; they tweaked their religion. Instead of sacrificing animals, they saw Jesus as the sacrifice for sins. However, they maintained the same legalism, although it was toned down from the extremism of the Pharisees. They are just as judgmental of those outside the tribe. To be honest, there is very little difference between a fundamentalist Christian and an Old Testament Jew. They both understand God in the same way. To both, Jesus says, "**Repent!**"

Appendix I:

Why Are Christians So Angry?

At the conclusion of a recent Bible study, a friend asked that we pray for our country, specifically mentioning the anger that is so prevalent. We see it all around us on social media, YouTube videos, road rage, and street protests. One of my first thoughts was that Christians are often out front in the anger parade. We are angry at many things.

Certain *sins* can really get us riled up, especially anything of a sexual nature. Christians fight against anything that smacks of homosexuality or gender identity. We're always quick to point out that we don't hate the sinner, just the sin. Abortion is another hot-button issue. Even the hint of not believing in banning every abortion will stir up the kind of anger that leads to war.

Many Christians also get angry over anything that even comes close to taking away freedom or rights. Don't dare suggest I wear a mask or get vaccinated because it might contribute to reducing the spread of a deadly virus. Freedom to carry guns is also a sacred right that causes many Christians to be angry when it is threatened. Christians often speak of *God-given rights* as if God actually gave us some rights.

There is no doubt that an anger problem exists among Christians. The question is why.

I have a suggestion, and it has nothing to do with our shameful culture, sinful world, or the approaching end times. The problem is God.

When God is angry, then God's people will be angry. Makes sense to me. And Christians have an angry God. God is *mad as hell* (literally) at sin. He is so angry that He is sending sinners to hell. In fact, we've always been taught that God is out to punish sinners. Yet, at the same time, God loves sinners, so He killed His own son instead. Consequently, sin gets punished by Jesus' sacrificial death, and everyone, including sinners, who believe in Jesus gets to go to heaven.

For centuries, men tried to offer animal sacrifices to atone for sin, but they proved inadequate. God's justice was so demanding and His wrath so intense that He required a perfect sacrifice, something more than a cow or a goat. He demanded a human, but no human was qualified. In steps Jesus, God's perfect Son, who jumped on the cross instead of us. God said, "I'm good with that, believe in Him, and you're ok."

It sounds rather crass when I write it like that, but that's what most of us have been taught over the years. Read parts of the Old Testament if you're not convinced that God is capable of great wrath. He is blamed for destroying entire cities in Canaan, drowning the Egyptian army, and every living person who was not one of Noah's kin. The Christian understanding that those who do not believe in Jesus are not saved means billions of people are doomed to spend eternity in endless torment.

If that's my God, can you blame me for being angry? It's understandable and justified.

But, here's the problem. We've also been taught that Jesus came to reveal God to us, to show us who God is, and to demonstrate God's love for us. Jesus wasn't angry at anyone. He wasn't mad at sinners; He wasn't interested in punishing sin. To be honest, sin didn't seem like such a big deal to Jesus. Let me tell you what I mean.

When they brought the sinful woman caught in the act of adultery to Jesus, He said, "Hey, I don't condemn you." Was He speaking for God at that point? When they lowered the paralyzed man through the roof, instead of healing his legs, Jesus forgave his sins without even being asked. He frequently dined with sinners. He specifically said he didn't come for the healthy; He came for the sinners. Sinners made up the crowds that surrounded Jesus.

When the disciples saw the man who had been blind from birth asked Jesus who had sinned, the man or his parents; Jesus said sin had nothing to do with it. Blindness was not a punishment. Or when the tower of Siloam fell (see Luke 13:4) and killed 18 people, it wasn't because of sin. Jesus was constantly correcting false beliefs about God. "You think God requires an eye for an eye, tooth for a tooth (retaliation). No! My Father wants you to turn the other cheek when slapped."

Any time you suggest that Jesus was not driven by anger, you will be confronted by His experience in the temple with the money changers. It's true; he made a whip and drove them out. Let me suggest a couple of things. None of the accounts indicate that He did it out of anger. Also, there is no suggestion that he harmed anyone, let alone caused them to die. It's nowhere near the type of anger that is blamed on God.

It's possible to be angry without lashing out. I recall a time when one of my teenage sons did something stupid, and I had to drive an hour and a half to pick him up and listen to a 30-minute lecture from a police sergeant. I couldn't say anything or defend either one of us because my son was at fault. To put it mildly, I was angry. It was a quiet ride home, and he knew I was angry. I didn't strike him or hurt him. I didn't make any ugly comments to him; I didn't need to; he got the message. To be honest, I don't think I even punished him. My anger was enough to solve the problem.

God might get angry at times, but He's nothing like us. He doesn't need to lash out and spew His anger. He has no need or desire to throw down lightning bolts or cause planes to fly into skyscrapers or hurricanes to destroy cities. That's not how He responds to sin. Jesus showed us how He responds to sin. He loves the sinner and shows a better way.

Jesus was not our substitute on the cross. There was no need for a substitute. God was not punishing sinners. God was loving sinners. That's why Jesus came. The reason He died on the cross is because we are threatened by the idea that God doesn't hate the people we hate, so we killed Him.

After Jesus brought Lazarus back to life, word spread like wild-fire. Listen to the response of the leaders: Therefore, the chief priests and the Pharisees convened a council meeting, and they were saying, "What are we doing in regard to the fact that this man is performing many signs? If we let Him go on like this, all the people will believe in Him, and the Romans will come and take over both our place and our nation." ... So from that day on they planned together to kill Him. (John 11:47-53)

Jesus didn't die to satisfy God's need for a sacrifice. He died because He challenged everything people valued. He turned their world upside down and threatened their existence. Yet here we are. Like the Pharisees and religious leaders of the first century, we're still angry at sinners and anyone who threatens our existence.

Christians are so angry because they still reject Jesus' message that God is not angry. Angry Christians behave as if Jesus' message was that you people better get your act together because God is mad as hell, and that's where He's sending you if you don't straighten up. If that's the way you understand God, then you can continue to be angry, but I choose not to serve that god.

Appendix II:

Off Course

When I set off to visit my neighbor across the street and plot a course directly to his front door, if I miscalculate by one degree, it's no big detail. Less than one step to the side will put me in the correct location. However, if I get on an airplane to fly a straight line from DFW to San Francisco with the same one-degree miscalculation, I will be at least 24 miles off target. The basic formula is every degree off course results in one mile for every 60 miles traveled. Imagine going around the world. Rather than returning to DFW, I would find myself somewhere in Kansas, perhaps near Kansas City.

Getting off to a good start is crucial. However, even the most accurate beginning can get off-target and need an occasional course correction. This same principle applies to decisions and time instead of distance and direction. If I make a decision that is not completely correct, the longer I continue with that decision, the more wrong I will be. I know that might sound a little confusing, but let me get to the point.

I think the church made a slightly incorrect decision at the beginning, and 2,000 years later, Christianity is far off target. The incorrect decision was to accept the Jewish scriptures (Old Testament) on an equal plane as the Gospel. The writers of the New Testament used the Scriptures (once again, the Old Testament) to demonstrate the legitimacy of Jesus—He is the Messiah the Jews had been seeking. Its value was pointing people to Jesus.

After the early apostles and church fathers disappeared from the scene, the church began reading the Old Testament differently. With the conversion of Constantine, he made an effort to use Christianity to legitimize his rule, which led to the marriage of church and state. That marriage grew stronger and stronger through history. Sometimes a strong Pope would give the church the upper hand. Occasionally, the church and state would see things differently. Perhaps one of the best known is when King Henry VIII couldn't get the church to do what he wanted, so he opened his own branch office.

Accepting the Old Testament on equal footing, or as many would say, equally inspired, with the New Testament has led to what many theologians call a *Flat Bible*. It means that all Scripture is equally valid. What Moses said is just as important as what Jesus said. The Book of Leviticus is as valuable as the Gospel of John. Now, I know you don't believe that. I don't think anyone believes that completely. However, many fail to understand that the Old Testament and New Testament are not compatible in a number of ways.

The Old Testament describes a God who is angry and judgmental and requires sacrifices for sin. The New Testament describes a God who loves us so much that He gave up His Son for our salvation. The Old Testament repeatedly explains how to make compensation for sin, even after repentance (see Psalm 51). The New Testament talks about forgiveness, even without repentance. The Old Testament requires restitution by those who have wronged another person. The New Testament encourages us to turn the other cheek. The list is endless. The Old Testament speaks of God striking people dead for certain offenses. The New Testament records Jesus speaking of forgiveness to those who crucified Him.

Preachers and scholars have become adept magicians practicing sleight of hand to convince us the Old Testament and New Testament are saying the same thing. If you don't believe the entire Bible is God-inspired, perfect, and without any error, then you are in danger of being ostracized by those in power. You've heard the old joke about the man who said he believed the Bible cover-to-cover; he even believed it was "genuine leather" and that the maps in the back were inspired.

This has created the problem that the New Testament is often interpreted based on what is in the Old Testament. That's backward. The correct position is that whenever the Old Testament contradicts the Gospel, the Old Testament is wrong.

Jesus frequently corrected the Old Testament. That's why the Pharisees had such problems with Him. He continually told them they were wrong, even though they lived according to the Old Testament, their Scripture. The most graphic example is when they brought the woman caught in adultery to Jesus. According to the Old Testament requirement, they were on their way to stone her and wanted Jesus' opinion. It's a great story, and Jesus essentially said God forgives her.

As strict followers of the Old Testament, the Pharisees could not recognize Jesus. In the Gospel of John, after Jesus healed the blind man, the Pharisees argued with the man and said, "We know that God has spoken to Moses, but as for this man (Jesus), we do not know where He is from" (John 9:29). Obviously, their Scriptures led them astray, yet the church came along and adopted those same Scriptures. Over time, those Scriptures came to have equal authority with the Gospel.

The early church got a little off target from the outset and began to view the Old Testament as more than a record of what God has done through history. It became a record of what He wanted to continue doing. Just a minor alteration. But that was 2,000 plus years ago, and today's church is far afield. They are approaching the airport in Kansas City instead of DFW.

These are some of the beliefs of a church that is off course:

- God sacrificed Jesus to appease His own anger over sin.
- God promised to bless His chosen nation. Since Israel does not follow Jesus, the U.S. is now His chosen nation, so we have Christian nationalism. Many take all the promises made to Israel as now promises to the U.S.

- It is necessary to keep God's commandments in order to be blessed by God. That's why legalism is so rampant among Christians.
- The standards of behavior required in the Old Testament haven't changed, so we need to condemn those who don't measure up, especially sexual attitudes.

Modern Christianity looks more like the Old Testament than it does Jesus:

- Hurling accusations at people
- Judging based on ethnicity
- Demanding adherence to strict rules of behavior
- Blaming tragedies on sin
- Requiring certain behaviors to be accepted by God
- Explaining suffering as the consequence of sin

We have come a long way from the Apostle Paul, who quoted the Old Testament to explain the existence of Jesus, or the writer of Hebrews, who described how Jesus superseded the Old Testament. Christians now believe that what Moses said can be just as binding as what Jesus said. Many problems with today's Christianity can be traced to the acceptance of an Old Testament concept instead of a New Testament revelation.

Jesus turned the religious world upside down with His understanding of God. What He taught was so different than what the Old Testament followers believed that they eventually had Him killed. Jesus didn't die to appease God, who required a sacrifice for sin. He died because He claimed that God forgives sin and didn't need a sacrifice.

Jesus began His ministry with a call to *repent*. Repentance is still needed when it comes to how we understand the Old Testament. It is a history of how men have related to God for thousands of years. It is a story of man's failure to understand God. It is not a guide for understanding, knowing, or relating to God. That was the work of Jesus.

www.ingramcontent.com/pod-product-compliance
Lightning Source LLC
Chambersburg PA
CBHW060401090426
42734CB00011B/2223